Theory for Theatre Studies: Movement

Theory for Theatre Studies meets the need for accessible, mid-length volumes that unpack keywords that lie at the core of the discipline. Aimed primarily at undergraduate students and secondarily at postgraduates and researchers, the volumes feature both background material historicizing the term and original, forward-looking research into intersecting theoretical trends in the field. Case studies ground volumes in praxis, and additional resources online ensure readers are equipped with the necessary skills and understanding as they move deeper into the discipline.

SERIES EDITORS

Susan Bennett, University of Calgary, Canada

Kim Solga, Western University, Canada

Theory for Theatre Studies: Movement

Rachel Fensham

Series editors: Susan Bennett and Kim Solga

methuen | drama

LONDON • NEW YORK • OXFORD • NEW DELHI • SYDNEY

METHUEN DRAMA
Bloomsbury Publishing Plc
50 Bedford Square, London, WC1B 3DP, UK
1385 Broadway, New York, NY 10018, USA

BLOOMSBURY, METHUEN DRAMA and the Methuen Drama logo are
trademarks of Bloomsbury Publishing Plc

First published in Great Britain 2021

Series design by Louise Dugdale
Cover image: Henrik Sorensen/Photodisc/Getty

A catalogue record for this book is available from the British Library.

A catalog record for this book is available from the Library of Congress.

ISBN:	HB:	978-1-3500-2637-7
	PB:	978-1-3500-2636-0
	ePDF:	978-1-3500-2639-1
	eBook:	978-1-3500-2638-4

Series: Theory for Theatre Studies

Typeset by Integra Software Services Pvt. Ltd.

To find out more about our authors and books visit www.bloomsbury.com
and sign up for our newsletters.

Zeno denied the existence of movement. By way of refutation, Diogenes the Cynic started to walk; and even had he been able only to limp, he would have made the same answer!

Denis Diderot, 1758

CONTENTS

SECTION TWO
Movement Systems and Embodied Action 77

SECTION THREE
Movement in Contemporary Theatre 135

SERIES PREFACE

Theory for Theatre Studies (TfTS) is a series of introductory theoretical monographs intended for both undergraduate and postgraduate students as well as researchers branching out into fresh fields. It aims to introduce constellations of ideas, methods, theories and rubrics central to the working concerns of scholars in theatre and performance studies at the opening of the twenty-first century. With a primary focus on twentieth-century developments, TfTS volumes offer accessible and provocative engagements with critical theory that inspire new ways of thinking theory in important disciplinary and interdisciplinary modes.

The series features full-length volumes explicitly aimed at unpacking sets of ideas that have coalesced around carefully chosen key terms in theatre and performance, such as space, sound, bodies, memory, movement, economies and emotion. TfTS volumes do not aggregate existing essays but rather provide a careful, fresh synthesis of what extensive reading by our authors reveals to be key nodes of interconnection between related theoretical models. The goal of these texts is to introduce readers to a wide variety of critical approaches and to unpack the complex theory useful for both performance analysis and creation.

Each volume in the series focuses on one specific set of theoretical concerns, constellated around a term that has become central to understanding the social and political labour of theatre and performance work at the turn of the millennium. The organization of each book follows a common template: Section One includes a historical overview of interconnected theoretical models, Section Two features extended case studies using twentieth- and twenty-first-century performances, and

Section Three looks ahead, as our authors explore important new developments in their constellation. Each volume is broad enough in scope to look laterally across its topic for compelling connections to related concerns, yet specific enough to be comprehensive in its assessment of its particular term. The ideas explored and explained through lively and detailed case studies provide diverse critical approaches for reading all kinds of plays and performances as well as starting points for practical exploration.

Each book includes a further reading section and features a companion website with chapter summaries, questions for discussion, and a host of video and other web links.

Susan Bennett (University of Calgary, Canada)
and Kim Solga (Western University, Canada)

ACKNOWLEDGEMENTS

My heartiest thank you belongs to the series editors, Susan Bennett and Kim Solga. First, for their invitation to write this book and for giving me a deadline, and secondly, for their patient and enthusiastic encouragement for the project. Their commitment to the series at Methuen Drama, and the support of publishers Mark Dudgeon and Lara Bateman, has been a strong incentive for a meaningful outcome.

I am grateful for research leave supported by the School of Culture and Communication at the University of Melbourne, and I can hear the voices of many teachers, colleagues and students from different institutions throughout the book. I would like to thank the anonymous reader who offered such encouraging but thought-provoking suggestions for the manuscript and editor Sally Moss who assisted with a first proof-read. And I want to express my warm appreciation of theatre colleagues and friends, Sarah Balkin and Sara Jane Bailes, who gave attentive, generous and critical feedback at crucial stages of the writing process. A final, but not least, thank you extends to my life companion and interlocutor Adrian Montana.

The inspiration of performers and artists is at the heart of this book, as they continue to complicate and evolve understandings of movement through their theatre. Writing this book with respect for their efforts, creativity and embodied politics has consistently moved my thinking about performance.

Movement: Introduction

A young woman is dancing, and she has a rapid and fluid style that includes folding in and out of the floor of the stage, lifting her arms and whirling around, lots of sideways torsion, with her long hair flying as if the final flick of the movement comes from deep within her. She wears dark, loose-fitting trousers and a top which folds around her, and the music carries her into what feels like a kind of trance. After about five minutes, another dancer appears, entering upstage left. He walks slowly but sensuously, bent slightly forward with neck extended as if he is paying attention to some intricate disturbance in his feet. He wears conventional masculine attire – a buttoned shirt and jeans, with no obvious concession to dance except the bare feet. As soon as he enters, it is hard not to take your eyes off him even though the younger dancer keeps moving.

In movement terms, one might say that she is all flow while he is entirely bound; moreover his movements carry weight and occupy time and space in an entirely different way from hers. The two dancers establish a distinct rhythmic dynamics in the performance where smooth abstract movements are punctuated by gestures that signify distinct attributes of each person. In 2017 when the Sadlers Wells theatre in London hosted the Elixir Festival, a programme of dance works created by 'senior' artists who have enjoyed exceptional dance careers and reputations,

I found myself attending to this duality of movement styles and affects. The work I have just described was a commission called *Songs of Childhood* choreographed by Pascal Merighi for Dominique and Thusnelda Mercy, which you may also like to watch on Vimeo.[1]

Through his long career as principal dancer with Pina Bausch's company, the Tanztheater Wuppertal, Dominique Mercy is well known, and if you have seen any of their productions on video or stage you might remember him in his suit, performing with a deadpan attitude, or in *Nelken* (1982) shouting at the audience in a black tutu. He is tall and aquiline, with an exquisite sense of timing and a consciously wry attitude towards his own virtuosity as an artist. Thusnelda is the daughter of Dominique and another Bausch dancer Malou Airaldo and hence grew up in the company and world of European dance as well as having her own training and opportunities to create performance. Her movements reflect the influence of different kinds of training systems, as well as an entirely different historical and social life experience. I do not know the biographical details but let us imagine a young French boy in the 1960s wanting to be a ballet dancer, and perhaps not from a dance family, and compare that with a young girl in the 1980s where dancing was part of her everyday in a country with liberal social norms. With a difference in age of about thirty years, the older person has a long history of observing the embodied movements of himself and others, as well as incorporating the struggles of his ballet training into choreographic structures, whereas the younger person conveys the energetic propulsions of an embodied imagination still forming.

Perhaps then it is not surprising that we see two different ways of moving on the stage at one time; the one loose and open, the other conscious and controlled. The contrasts are compelling but what do they represent? How do different kinds of technique habituate the body to a repertoire of movement, and how does that shape and contribute to a performance aesthetic? The stripped back form – bare stage, minimal costumes, trained bodies – of the dance example suggests that movement can be constituted by macro- and micro-levels of attention at one and the same time, with its extension – spatial, rhythmic, haptic – into the world around the self. What is important at the outset of this book on theories of movement in theatre is that we pay attention to how movement functions across a range of registers that become essential to the experience of the work.

With its focus on theatre rather than dance, this book aims to explore a range of aesthetic, social and philosophical ideas about theatre movement in historical terms and to see how theories of movement have emerged in specific contexts and alongside contemporary understandings of movement practices in the theatre. In theatre history, while dramatic theories shaped the study of literary genres such as tragedy and comedy, and psychological theories have examined acting, authenticity and the study of emotion in theatre, there is unfortunately no equivalent body of writings on movement for theatre. So we will attempt to extract a range of theories from the workings of theatre practices with two guiding approaches to theory for theatre. Firstly, the eminent theatre scholar Marvin Carlson suggests that theories of drama include 'statements of general principles regarding the methods, aims, function, and characteristics of this particular art form', thus separated, on the one hand, from aesthetics, dealing with art in general, and, on the other, from the criticism of particular works and reviews of particular productions (1984: 9). Such 'general principles' of theatre theory rarely exist in a pure form, however, since these observations are embedded in or related to forms and modes of expression in other arts, such as sculpture, design, dance and music. A second framing of theory is offered by a recent study of the Greek chorus and suggests that when we investigate theatre we are involved in processes 'of conceptualizing, of suggesting and shaping perceptions and interpretations about a given phenomenon' (Peponi 2013: 16). In both approaches, theatre theory relies on a grounded methodology, whereby our suggestions and interpretations of movement might be articulated gradually, intimately and critically in relation to the formation of distinctive aspects of theatrical experience.

The approach of this book is thus selective about the historical framing of the topic and indeed conscious of the limitations of thinking about movement from any one cultural position. We ask, then, what questions might be, or should be, posed and answered by a book on theories of movement for theatre? What is movement? Who or what is being moved and how? And which movements are felt, observed or studied in theatre? Or more precisely following from the example above, in what ways do the learned and specialized techniques of performing bodies contribute to understandings of social and political understandings of movement? How do we distinguish between movement that is intrinsic to an individual and that which is constructed for theatre itself? And what kind of movements could be included in a broad theatrical repertoire – the movement of bodies, animals, plants and objects? Or, do we follow the movement of the event as a whole, such as the durational and spatial aspects of the entire stage world? These questions suggest investigations that apply as much to the individual (actor or spectator) as they do to the collective experience of a social body. For instance, the German word *bewegung*, while generally meaning 'motion' in the physical sense, is also used to refer to a political movement. Movement in this expanded sense is that which mobilizes or implies motion. Movement is thus neither uniquely human nor uniquely sentient; it can exist in other objects and things that move, whether as abstract ideas or observable realities. While theatre often manipulates that which is observable and known, through the movement of actors, it also conjures with what is not seen and is less well known. As we progress through the book, these questions will thicken and expand the repertoire of ideas we have about how movement matters to the communication and experience of performance.

Before we delve more deeply into 'statements of general principles' or the 'shaping perceptions' of movement in association with examples of theatre in context, this introduction will address three concepts that inform the theorization of movement throughout this book. The first is that of movement as a property of life force, or the animations of the soul, that the Greek philosopher Aristotle pondered more than two thousand years ago. The second is the notion of difference in movement, understood through techniques of the body, which became important in the anthropological writing of Marcel Mauss in the early twentieth century when he began to consider the intercultural aspects of bodily movements, attitudes and behaviours. And the third is the concept of rhythm, which according to Henri LeFebvre, has an important sociological dimension. Rhythm represents a critical term in the patterning of space-time in social relations and perhaps also for understanding the larger dynamics of day-night, weather, ecosystems and cosmological spheres.

Vital beings: Aristotle

In Aristotle's book *De Anima* (Soul, or Spirit), the mystery of movement – of humans, animals, elements and things – is a central preoccupation: 'For how are we to understand a unit as being in movement? By what is it moved, and in what way, since it is partless and undifferentiated. For insofar as it is capable of moving things and of being moved, it must admit of differentiation' (Aristotle 2017: 15). Aristotle's investigation of these questions echoes my own fascination with how things are modified over time and in space, and he answers them with mathematics and with rhythm, with breath and passion, and above all with what he calls spirit (anima), or the evidence of the 'soul in nature'. Thinking about movement in philosophy is therefore to enquire into the properties of movement as animate existence and to wonder about the distinction between things that are active, those that are at rest and those that have passive capacities – all the while recognizing that the boundaries between different bodies are subject to continuous change.

Scholarly study of his treatise, *The Poetics*, most referenced in relation to theatre has concentrated on the philosophical and structural principles of tragic form and their impact on an audience and we will consider Aristotle's conception of the chorus in Section One. Carlson cautions that 'interpretation of key concepts' in *The Poetics* has however been based on the fragments of ancient texts and therefore need to be cross-referenced against other sources (1984: 16). My reading of movement theories in Aristotle's other writings, such as the *Physics* and *De Anima*, is therefore intertextual with *The Poetics* and considers that his teaching may have assumed knowledge of key ideas between these volumes. Theories about the movement of physical properties, object or animal corporeality, and the evidence of 'soul', for instance, might also inform our thinking about performance.

In the *Physics*, motion in an object resembles or demonstrates change, such as that exists in a transition between two points. A ball or cart will travel forward until something stops moving the object and it becomes stationary. The object was here and is now there, so his primary question becomes, what initiates movement? The physical properties of movement include the forces that made the object move, whether a body part, such as legs, or an inhuman thing such as wind. That a moving thing is caused by some agency is most evident in things that are moved contrary to nature, perhaps resistant to moving, since they must be moved by something external. Then there is the puzzle of things that, by nature, move themselves – for example, animals. Movement can be provoked, either by 'nature' (conceived of as intrinsic to a body, not as the organic world) or by 'force' (some external agency), and likewise rest can occur in nature or by force (energy being arrested).

But does the human being move in ways that are different either from other animals or from other material objects, or indeed from more celestial and abstract things? In D. C. Reeve's recent translation of *De Anima*, human movement becomes ontological: what moves us, and how are we moved, whether by the soul or incorporeal things? In a most logical way, Aristotle assesses the experience of movement, and the kinesthesia of 'being moved', in relation to the perception, imagination, desire and understanding of the anima (the soul) (Aristotle 2017: 124, n201). He defines this sensation of movement as 'the potentiality of an actuality', two key principles of animation which suggest performance, since a potentiality motivates all dramatic action and narrative (2017: 21, 30–1). In an exciting way, this idea of motion resembles contemporary conceptions of movement that affirm the potentiality of a person's becoming rather than demand or delimit the being of the self in the world. But how does potentiality shape the actuality of physical movement with all its implications for corporeal expression and understanding?

Aristotle expands this conception of movement by proposing four types of motion: 'spatial movement, alteration, withering and growth' (2017: 9). Having approached the concept of the spatial as movement between two points, or the displacement of a body or object, alteration is a more abstract conception of movement whereby a thing or a concept is altered, perhaps by the effects of time; by contrast, withering is related to the process of dying and decay, while the growth of an organic object moves by a shift in capacity through age or maturation. Movement thus can be assessed as mathematical or topological, as well as organic or affective, with the latter understood as changes in *energeia* (relating thus to the Chinese concept of *chi* or spirit). This concept of movement as energy flow includes recognition of breath; the elements (parts) that make up the body; and the animating power of knowledge, from which Aristotle concludes that the 'soul' comprises three attributes: moving, perceiving and being incorporeal, that is, not entirely within the visible realm (2017: 8). Most importantly, relations with perceptible objects, formed in imagination, assist the soul to move, to change and to actualize a probability. Imagine, for instance, the differences in a lion seizing its prey or an old man navigating the stairs, and think of them as probable motivations for movement.

This ontological relationship between soul and movement is complex, and Aristotle attempts to determine whether the 'soul' moves the body or whether the body and its sensations – its perceptible objects – animate the soul. In a sense, he tries to understand what is intrinsic to human 'nature' (that which makes us distinctive in our knowledge of ourselves and our place in the sensory world). He keeps wondering if the answer lies in physics, in the senses, in the elements, in parts of the body, or in human motivation. Let me draw out just a couple of features that pertain to theorization of movement in and for the theatre: namely, the affective content of movement and the binding properties of the soul, which involve the 'actualisation of a certain sort of body' (Aristotle 2017: 25).

Refuting Plato, who regarded the soul as more or less the stable centre of a harmonic universe, Aristotle argues that the soul cannot 'revolve in a circle', since it takes the soul or subject back to its starting point. Instead, 'movement is the activity of what is incomplete' (2017: 431). The perceptions and recollections that are the property of the soul will leave us 'pained, enjoying, feeling confident, feeling afraid, and, further, [is] feeling angry and also perceiving and thinking. And all of these seem to be movements' (2017: 14). The actor or spectator who perceives the stage as a place to watch the various pains of the soul in all its incompleteness may be in furious agreement with Aristotle's expanded idea of the soul as a complex of affects, being moved. He, however, refuses to be satisfied with either the physical or affective propositions he has developed for understanding movement. Rather, he asks what role recollection might play for the soul and thus how the traces of movement in the perceptual organs affect our understanding? This is what we would today call cognition, the mental processing of our sensory responses to or from motor activity. Hence we may perceive movement but the neural networks in the body and brain must also recall its traces for a particular physical sensation to have an effect on knowledge.

Beyond perception and the accumulation of knowledge, Aristotle also wants to understand how movements of the spirit might be linked with desire or the will to move the body. Slowly he disentangles knowledge from mere affects, and soul from the physical body, not because he is interested in a disembodied self but because movement for him also comprises the desired experience of movement as much as what happens physically or to the material object. Thus how we imagine movement becomes part of the experience of self: 'So is it reasonable that these two things – desire and practical thought – appear to be the causes of movement ... what causes movement in every case is the object of desire, which is the good or the apparent good – not every good, however, but the good that is doable in action' (Aristotle 2017: 61). This seems to be a very contemporary argument that doing things – making actions to move or instigate movement – can be both practical as well as a desirable wish for change, growth and displacement.

What binds these principles of movement – 'holds them all together' – is understanding: the means we have of synthesizing and reflecting upon the movement of perceptible objects, whether sensorial or imaginary forms, which allows the 'soul' to comprehend good from bad, like from unlikeness, and thus to differentiate. The importance of desire and the place of physical 'passion' (defined as the intensification of pleasure and pain) in the actions of a performance are it seems articulated in this reading of Aristotle. Such a conception of movement, or vital force, has engaged theorists from Aristotle to Thomas Aquinas, Gottfried Wilhelm Leibniz to Isaac Newton, Henri Bergson to Alva Noë. While Aristotle's writings underpin this tradition, they also connect with contemporary perspectives on consciousness which stress that movement is a distinctive aspect of knowing and imagining – what Aristotle calls the probability of an actuality – which resides in the differences between stillness and action, thought and mere propulsion. Let us think now less universally about how movement might be differentiated by culture and experience in the writings of Marcel Mauss.

Bodily technique: Mauss

The French sociologist Marcel Mauss gave a series of lectures in the 1930s in which he noted the habituation of 'techniques of the body' in diverse cultures. Influenced by the expansive field of structural anthropology, he proposed that differences in ordinary bodily movement between genders, racial and national groups might be considered 'techniques' – that is, bodily movements that are not natural but rather acquired and learned actions. In his observation there are a multiplicity of hidden or unconscious 'techniques' or systems of movement organization that play out across all human activity including the particularities of 'non-movement': 'Techniques of activity, of movement. By definition, rest is the absence of movements, movement the absence of rest' (1979: 81).

For Mauss, differentiating problematically between races and classes, such a system of difference becomes inscribed by through the efficiency or 'dexterity' with which an individual acts and performs a specific technique, whether climbing, sitting, cleaning teeth or having sex. Mauss's description of the distinctive features of 'Walking' is telling:

> The habitus of the body being upright while walking, breathing, rhythm of the walk, swinging the fists, the elbows, progression with the trunk in advance of the body or by advancing either side of the body alternately (we have got accustomed to moving all the body forward at once). Feet in or out. Extension of the leg.
>
> (Mauss 1979: 82)

By regarding movement stylization as neither intrinsic to nor the distinct property of an individual, Mauss began to consider 'the work of psycho-sociological taxonomy' embodied through processes of imitation and education. Importantly, he considered the uniqueness of individual subjectivity to be less important than the social formation of movement habits that include the physical and disciplining practices generalized by a society. The detailed ensemble of movement practices acquired as 'walking' is thus adapted by social and historical contingencies – and this bodily repertoire can change inter-generationally as well as cross-culturally. Mauss appraises this idea when he sees the women of Paris adopting ways of walking 'like American girls'. This kind of observation of subtle differences in the use of weight, orientation, open and closed use of joints or body parts, and the general rhythmic semantics of an action, rehearsed in everyday movements, remains important for studying movement in theatre. If you observe classmates or walkers in the street, how many different ways can an actor construct a walk? Is the body upright? Do the arms swing or not? What is the lean of the torso relative to head and hips? Are the feet parallel or slightly splayed? And is the step wide and long, or short and skipping? Beyond identifying how we copy movement from parents or friends, Mauss proposes that specific systems of training, such as those that take place in sport, can lead to a more effective movement repertoire; for instance, we save energy by not undertaking superfluous movements, such as flapping our hands, but in organizing these component parts, we also constitute recognized social traits. Social and mental life, according to Mauss, is a sophisticated movement apparatus that includes 'a retarding mechanism, a mechanism inhibiting disorderly movements; ... [which] allows a co-ordinated response of coordinated movements setting off in the direction of a chosen goal' (1979: 86). Otherwise we would all walk with the ungainly steps of a toddler.

Such a purposeful sense of movement increasing efficiency and being learned within social and cultural contexts has had enormous influence on twentieth century, or modernist, approaches to systems of training within theatre as we will see in Section Two. As I suggested in the opening example, it also means that we may recognize different stylizations of learned techniques within the aesthetics of one performance. Mauss's astute reflections on the alternations between rest and activity also offer an interpretative framework for understanding movement as a social schema, which have a bearing on critiques of movement essentialism; the social coding of mobility, comportment and kinaesthesia expertise needs thus to be examined as one of the regulatory mechanisms controlling class, gender, race and ability. Awareness of techniques of movement requires us to contest cultural assumptions about how different bodies perform ordinary tasks while asking us to acknowledge that theatre and dance techniques extend beyond the known of Western traditions and movement practices. Our enjoyment of, and interaction with, diverse bodily patterns of movement can therefore be aided by analysis of the social organization of corporeal habits and training.

Rhythm: Lefebvre

The sociologist Henri Lefebvre spent much of his life thinking about the social production of space; however, his last book *Rhythmanalysis: Space, Time and Everyday Life* (2004) reflects on the elusive notion of social time. Rhythm, of course, reintroduces timing into the study of theatre, alongside bodies and space, and of course, the temporality of movement is of interest and significance to much contemporary theatre as we shall see in Section Three.

Lefebvre begins with an Aristotelian set of definitions, first of all by identifying rhythm with metre, that is the space between one point and another, revealing the often regular, patterned segments in which a displacement occurs. Metre implies measure, which suggests a quantifiable difference between one action and another. From measure, with repetition, pattern emerges so that we can identify a sequence or a connection between one measure and another. As with Mauss, but here in more abstract terms, pattern admits of qualitative variation.

Everywhere where there is interaction between a place, a time and an expenditure of energy, there is rhythm. Therefore:

a) repetition (of movements, gestures, action, situations, differences);

b) interference of linear processes and cyclical processes;

c) birth, growth, peak, then decline and end. (Lefebvre 2004: 25)

On the one hand, formulaic equations express the quantities of difference that define rhythm, and on the other, the processual transformations of rhythm lead to an elaborate artistic repertoire of processes that resemble the rising and falling of life itself. Rhythmic interactions which involve such patterns of 'repetition' and 'interference' can be realized when the predictable and disjunctive aspects of rhythm invite experimentation in theatre.

Case Study: *1980* (1980), *Bandoneon* (1981)

The Introduction began with description of two dancers associated with the choreographer Pina Bausch so this case study will examine how rhythm features in her genre of dance-theatre. Her theatricality is often attributed to her evocative imagery and the potent use of her dancers' stories to generate what 'moves them'. Musicality and rhythm are also distinctive features of her genre of dance-theatre perhaps so omnipresent that one almost fails to notice them, except perhaps when the music stops and gestures continue into silence. Let us look briefly at some short examples where the concept of rhythm exceeds the specificity of the performers' crafted technique and becomes a pattern or metaphor for something more complex than mere representation.

As a choreographer, Bausch's sense of rhythm was, of course, orchestrated by an advanced repertoire of dance techniques and spatial stylization of the mise en scène. *1980* (1980) was a work filled with mourning and loss after the death of her husband, and I recall seeing a line of dancers performing a strange, repetitive sequence of hand gestures: stroking the sides of their torso, clasping hands, flicking a clenched fist sideways, and pushing something over the shoulder. In Bausch's biography, Marion Meyer recalls this sequence differently: 'the dancers ... wipe the tears from their cheeks and clap their hands gently ... [they] also come together in pairs or dance their way through the auditorium in a trademark line' (2017: 76). Counted neatly to four beats and accompanied by the elegant Bausch walk – long legs fully extended in a slow strolling pattern, torso upright – the dancers' tilted heads express a somewhat supercilious, or perhaps insouciant, smile. Rhythms such as these both reveal and hide the sense of sadness and as Lefebvre suggests, performance gets entwined through a rhythmic coding that is both 'secret (recollection and memory, the said and unsaid)' and very 'public (therefore social)' (2004: 27). The memory impressions of this rhythmic utterance are difficult to interpret, but insofar as the peculiar gestures carry the rhythm of the music, such knowledge remains 'simultaneously banal and full of surprises' (Lefebvre 2004: 77).

Lefebvre's concept of rhythmanalysis, used here as a theory for theatre, includes more than organic movements, learned habits or the measured organization of rhythmic gesture, such as the *1980* dance sequence illustrates. From Lefebvre, we learn that rhythm is more complex than eurythmics, which is the study of harmony, or isorhythmia, in which different rhythms have equal value. He attributes a social dimension to the effects of force, arguing that 'once one discerns relations of force in social relations and relations of alliance one perceives their link with rhythm. Alliance supposes harmony between different rhythms, conflict supposes arrhythmia: a divergence in time, in space, in the use of energies' (2004: 79). As anyone knows when they wake someone from sleep, we are not all in sync with one another all of the time. Further appreciation of the great diversity of rhythmic structures includes polyrhythms that appear simultaneously at different tempi or across different strata, as well as arrhythmia, in which rhythms break apart, alter and bypass synchronization – and such recognized, yet complex patterns can inform movement composition in theatre.

This sophisticated attunement to localized rhythmic patterns can be used to invigorate theatre creation. In another Bausch example, *Bandoneon* (1981), which followed from her ensemble's tour to Argentina, evokes the music and dynamics of the tango. As soon as two dancers take up the opening couple position, the audience imagines the sound of the sliding guitar and the probability of the dance even without actually seeing it. Following a rehearsal process of questioning about 'love' and memories of yearning, the dancers' personal 'stories become alternative cues, and movement codes' that punctuate the performance (Hoghe 2016: 102). Within one sequence called 'suicide game', dancers describe a minor childhood affliction and then 'jump' from any platform or ledge they can find. Counterpointed with the alternation of increasingly grim, death-defying anecdotes, a solo dancer continues her 'ballet practice, undeterred' while another sings a cheerful kindergarten song. The intertwining of these three rhythms – the bursts of jumping, the repetitions of a learned dance and a cute melody – exerts a kind of fatalistic tension, whereby the innocent playfulness of childhood becomes the macabre pattern for an unfulfilled adult life. Another dimension of rhythm appears through the choice of music, but also indirectly in what Lefebvre calls a 'garland of rhythms' without for a moment imagining that all of life is flowers (2004: 30). Bausch herself offers a valuable reflection on her own assemblage of these rhythmic garlands: 'A moment where something is one thing and something else, where two worlds collide' (cited in Hoghe 2016: 108).

Many theatre artists create performances that utilize a heightened consciousness of rhythm – using counts, beats or diverse tempi – whether in a West End show or in a small studio work, when they are navigating the complexity of rhythm in the body, in the score or text, in the everyday, and in the uses of timing and space. If however we conceive of rhythm as a highly patterned relationality, which establishes the time zones required for movements to traverse between bodies, clusters of meaning and social groups, then the densely patterned actuality of theatre as a movement in time, as much as space, becomes foregrounded and this is an important addition to our thinking about movement in theatre.

About this book

From Aristotle, Mauss and Lefebvre, we have acquired some ideas about how movement allows perceptible objects to become known and thus for the conscious self to cultivate or acquire techniques that activate the potential of change over space and time. This sense of movement as an objective reality can represent and be embodied as the spirit life, the physical nature of things and the sociality of the subject. Many different societies locate movement analogies in parts of the body, such as breath (lungs), pulse (heart) or core/desire (solar plexus). Others rely upon metaphors from the mechanics of objects, such as balls, cars, clocks and planes. Hence, responding to movement becomes a form of corporeal intelligence, a potentiality that exists alongside the material and perceptible sense of personhood in a specific time and place. Differentiation of movement repertoires is what stimulates our perception, imagination, cognition and memory; hence all of these are in play within a theatre performance.

In theatre studies, as we will see, other ideas of movement are also important such as the relationship between movement and action, and the circulation of energy and ideas. Even when movement knowledge becomes transmitted imperceptibly, for instance, via technology, the probabilities of theatre movement test the limits of action in both theatre and the non-theatrical world. This book will locate its theories within specifics, such as theatre genres, diverse cultures or distinctive productions. The first two sections of the book are historical, while the last section attends to a selection of key ideas from contemporary theatre. All the sections narrate accounts of individual and movement formations that belong to groups, as well as attempting to consider and affirm the intercultural aspects of an increasingly transnational, hybrid theatre culture.

Section One is dedicated to a broad trans-historical view stretching from the fifth century BC to the eighteenth century. It considers the difference between the movement of the chorus and that of the actor within different social contexts – from Greek theatre to the medieval religious procession, and from the Japanese court to Renaissance spectacle. This section strives to understand how ideas about movement in relation to the stage are connected to the history of social life, whether through the power of rhetoric or reason. It also records the richness of movement theories produced by theatre itself – by practitioners – during periods in which theatre was a major medium of cultural expression and influence. It includes case studies of a production of *Antigone* by the Japanese theatre director Satoshi Miyagi, *The Tempest* by William Shakespeare, as well as the examples of *Zero Degrees*, an intercultural dance-theatre production; *I Am My Own Wife*, a contemporary play that tests the limits of gestural intelligibility; and the blockbuster production, *War Horse*.

Section Two focuses on twentieth-century developments that have informed enduring ideas of movement in theatre, such as that of plasticity, dynamics and the esoteric. While being considered as artistic terms, these ideas have been underpinned by intellectual discourses that extend the references between the work of art and social reality. Scientific or structuralist approaches to knowledge have thus led to 'systems' that enhance and transmit movement in theatre, from the training of actors to the uses of technology and stagecraft. The section recognizes the role of significant twentieth-century theatre practitioners, from Stanislavski, Brecht, Meyerhold, Laban, Grotowski to Ohno who have transformed understanding of the actor's physical movement, and provides case studies from the modern theatrical works, *Hedda Gabler*, *Mother Courage* and *The Constant Prince*; examples from Butoh performance as well as a reworking of the chorus by contemporary companies, such as Hotel Pro Forma and Oentroerend Goed.

Section Three identifies a selection of concepts with currency in twenty-first-century theory useful to the study of theatre, theatre criticism and analysis, such as speed, stillness, animation and force. New ideas are emerging all the time, so theatre productions always present us with the challenge of 'theorizing', extending from the particular to the generalizable – even when what we experience in the theatre is frustratingly difficult to explain. Analogous concepts are often productive particularly if we want to acknowledge our own blind spots, and those cultural biases that might misrepresent movement histories or knowledges. The perspective of non-white, non-binary, and diversely abled bodies and individuals is transformative of theatre and includes a redistribution of the power of movement. Case studies in this section include a production of Martin Crimp's *Attempts on Her Life*; Marina Abramović, in her performance, *The Artist Is Present*, as well as new works, *World Factory* by the Chinese theatre company Grass-Stage and UK company Metis; a German-Bangladeshi co-production, *Made in Bangladesh*; and an Australian Indigenous production, *Blackie Blackie Brown* by Nakkiah Lui.

SECTION ONE

Movement as History

Movement is that most fleeting of attributes – a twitch of the nostrils, a bold dash from one corner to another, or the strange flickering of a light source – and we register all these qualitative differences as the very vitality and evocation of being present at the theatre. This present tense of movement as an energetic field, contingent on what is changing, makes it difficult to appreciate how movement might have shaped theatre history. We temptingly want to ask not only who was there, but also how did the performers or audience actually move? Were actors of another era stiff and robotic, or fluent and naturalistic? And, by what means, physical or mechanical, were the stage effects of movement rendered? Thinking about times before recording devices could capture movement as a temporal phenomenon, how can we appreciate the ways in which embodied actions communicated? These questions suggest that movement and history might be antithetical; however, while we cannot become participants in a past event, there are indirect methods – in texts, pictures, diagrams, philosophies and embodied experience – that help us to consider how movement was practised and conceptualized by different theatre traditions. By examining how movement genres arose in specific places, as we will do in this section, we can try to understand how the motility of theatre provides a way to understand the complexity of history.

I will approach this topic by adopting a global history approach which examines the connectivity and diversity of theatre histories around the world, such as between the ancient Greek orchestra and Noh theatre, or from Roman rhetoric to Indian acting theory; as well as a scalar approach, attentive to the interdependence between big and small examples, ranging from medieval processions and grand Renaissance spectacle to the micro-manipulations of the puppet. This section considers theories that recognize the influence of movement upon audience reception, while paying attention to the social and ideological contexts which shape movement ideas – whether from religious or moral prejudice or from the science of the automaton – in theatre.

The chorus: Ancient Greek theatre

From architectural remains, we know that the ancient Greek stage was comprised of an *orchestra* – the open space in front of a *skena*, or scene (staging), that affords maximum visibility to the audience. Without illustrations, however, it is difficult to imagine the quality and experience of choral movement: how did the assembled company enter and exit, who were they, and how did they contribute to the action of the play? The philosophers tell us that they admired the chorus's role within theatre and social conduct. For Plato, the art of *choreia* was a practice of choral dancing and singing to be embraced by the well-educated (2014: 654b), and we know from Aristotle's *Poetics* that 'choral parts, comprising entry-song and ode' were 'common to all tragedies' (Aristotle 1996: 19–20), but also that 'one should handle the chorus as one of the actors; it should be a part of the whole and should contribute to the performance' (30). While detailed analysis of acting styles has rarely been the focus of Hellenic dramatic theory, it is evident that group movement must have accompanied the action in most productions. Recent scholarship, drawing upon archaeology, art history and music scholarship, examines both the theory and practices of the chorus, and Greek scholar Anastasia-Erasmia Peponi argues that 'both poetic and philosophical evidence indicates that in choral practices the alliance of body and voice was considered essential to the group's overall coordination, even in cases where the performance seemed to require a distribution of the kinetic and the vocal action between its members' (2013: 16). This contention about the centrality of the chorus is my starting point for a theory of movement in theatre: that what the chorus embodies as it moves, and as importantly, what affects it produces kinaesthetically, atmospherically and socially are central to understanding how theatre communicates. Indeed, I often play a game with myself when watching contemporary theatre productions with only a handful of actors as I try to imagine who the absent chorus might be and what they would be doing. Take for example a domestic drama in which a married couple are arguing about the wife's affair. Who would the chorus be here? Perhaps it is a group of women defending her right to an independent sexuality, or a group of children who lament their mother's neglect and the consequences of a broken-down home, or the noise of a workplace which has sucked both parents dry with its demands on their time. And as a chorus, they could at different times amplify and embody the energies of all three. You can therefore begin to picture what a greater mass of bodies carries within the action of a production, to grasp what social world these absent figures represent, and how their rhythm and weight would affect the dramaturgical impact of the performance.

Instructed to perform by the *choropheia* (the ensemble director commissioned by the festival playwright), the Greek theatre chorus was on a continuum with ritual and folk forms known from outlying villages to the streets of Athens. These performers could sing, dance and recite the stories of the gods and their lyric movements became important to the more formal emergence of theatre in urban society. With between fifteen and fifty performers used by different playwrights, the chorus would play multiple roles during the Greek theatre festivals that would last from day until night over three weeks each year. As a theory of the chorus however, Aristotle's delineation of dramatic structure through the vocal interactions of the chorus has been primary:

> The prologue is the whole part of a tragedy before the entry-song of the chorus; an episode is a whole part of the tragedy between whole choral songs; the finale is the whole part of the tragedy after which there is no choral song. Of the choral part, the entry-song is the first whole utterance of a chorus; an ode is a choral song without anapaests or trochaics; a dirge is a lament shared by the chorus and from the stage.
>
> (1996: 20)

One can easily imagine the prologue, the *parode*, and final speech, the *exode*, as forms of direct address to the audience in which the scale of the chorus makes an impression. What follows the prologue, however, must fill the stage with dynamic movement – anapaests and trochaic measures which become 'lively and full of motion' – whereas later choral segments might combine gestures with step patterns that respond to the narrative action.

For Aristotle, the rhythm of dancing that emanates from 'nature' is something all human beings have knowledge of in daily life and through ritual, dance and worship; however, the poetics of drama enhances these qualities through the 'extraneous efforts' of creativity and craft, or 'making' (1996: 7). As the genre of drama matured, the form and function of the Greek chorus developed close attention to the technique, rehearsals and preparation of movement required for the theatre. Aristotle alludes to this professionalization when he explains that performance 'generated poetry out of improvised activities by a process of gradual innovation' (1996: 7). The structure in which a soloist led and responded to a chorus is also recognizable as an improvised call and response in contemporary musical genres, such as gospel music, rock and hip-hop. In dramaturgical terms, the distinction between the actor as speaking subject and the movement of the whole led to the possibility of extended dialogue, although as the number of actors gradually increased from one to three, with more individualized characters supporting the dialogue, the role of the chorus began to decline in effectiveness.

Writing about variable approaches to the role of the chorus, whether 'cooperating with the players' or singing as 'interludes', Aristotle never discounted the role of the chorus in shaping the impact of performance (1996: 30–1). His jibe against Euripides for using the chorus as spectacle in favour of Sophocles's more restrained approach suggests that the theory of the chorus continued to evolve as dramatic structures became adapted by different playwrights. Using the chorus to 'engage in a great deal of movement' to amuse the audience, rather than be denounced, seems a legitimate response to different conditions or purpose (1996: 46). Moreover, as recent scholarship suggests, the theatrical diversity of the chorus enables an 'interrogation of the ideological as well as the real boundaries between chorus and dance, between processionary and stationary choruses, between rehearsed and impromptu choruses, and so on' (Billings et al. 2013: 4). In social terms, these diverse workings of the chorus in Greek drama make explicit the tension between individuals and the embodiments of gods and rulers, as well as mobilizing the milieu in which a concept of community or body politics resides.

Briefly introduced by Aristotle in *The Poetics*, his discussion of rhythm, metre and harmony alludes to their movement potential on stage. Differences between the use of rhythm and metre are roughly translated as patterns of repetitive phrasing, leading to musicality, while metre (or measure) encodes the movement of feet, literally the anapaests, as well as the stresses placed upon words and phrases in speech. Vocality and physical expression become literally and poetically, in step with one another, when he claims 'the movement that properly belongs to the feet is walking, and this is the movement that properly belongs to humans' (Aristotle 2017: 9).

Even simple contrasts lead to a potentially infinite rhythmic progression. One might imagine here two facing lines of actors who simultaneously but in opposition lean forwards and back. This pulse creates an atmosphere that can be maintained with slight variations in tempo and weight and yet over time, say ten minutes, such a rhythmic exchange will establish a shared feeling of attunement as if the bodies move in a wider harmonic sphere. The forms of musicality which involve both melody and rhythm produce the effect of metre such as counting '1 and 2 and ... ', whereby shifting or displacement from one note or tone to another becomes the pattern-making of harmony. Music alone does not give rise to movement however; Aristotle observes that 'dance uses rhythm by itself and without melody (since dancers imitate character, emotion and action by means of rhythm expressed in motion)' (1996: 4). Thus it remains for actors, or dancers, to produce anima (soul) by figuring out the rhythms of their dancing feet in the drama. Aristotle importantly addresses these experiential aspects and qualities of movement, such as noting that rhythm is a craft embodied in practice and that modes of walking are a distinctive attribute of 'spirit', as much as breathing. These stresses of the anapaest – with its implied ebb and flow – inspire the slow progression of the chorus around a walled lake in the case study of Antigone that follows shortly.

In the *Poetics*, the more elusive concept of harmony features as a musical device, linked to the uses of metre in verse, but in *De Anima*, Aristotle makes finer distinctions: 'Harmony ... [could be] the ratio of things that are mixed together'; however, perceptible things are more complicated than a simple ratio or combination of parts, which will be 'many and various' (2017: 13). Harmony is not then a kind of singing that produces a sweet balance between two forms of movement or melody but, rather, includes multitudes of different voices or forces interacting with one another. Unless animated by movement, there is no harmony.

While many dramatic theories stem from the interplay between classical readings of tragedy (focusing on the role of actors, mimesis, unities of plot with time and place), Aristotle's theories of choral movement as sketched here may expand the imaginative horizon of theatre. A theory of the chorus as movement will consider the workings of bodies who might unify the parts as a 'whole' or provide harmonic contrasts to the dramatic action. If the chorus must convey both action and mood, alongside representation, the 'figured rhythms' of dancing will enter into the narrative transmission of affect and communal experience of Greek theatre. Such relations between rhythm and the chorus in ancient theatre become particularly potent when we look at classical texts in contemporary performance. Before examining a chorus in a contemporary case study of Sophocles's *Antigone* produced by a Japanese director, I want to digress through the precise vocabulary of stage movement in the Japanese tradition of Noh theatre. This discussion extends theories of the chorus to the qualities of movement to be attained in the preparation of individual actors.

'The flower': Japanese Noh

With strong formal aesthetics and ritualized practices that invoke the relations between gods and humans, comparisons are usefully made between ancient Greek theatre and Noh (Smethurst 2013). Noh theatre is however still practised today and can be seen at dedicated outdoor theatres in Kyoto and Tokyo among other places. In contrast with studying an advanced theatrical form preserved by a few plays, philosophical texts and artefacts, Noh provides a continuous performance history with a detailed literary tradition and extant dramatic theory. The classical theatre form of Noh flourished in Japan in the fourteenth and fifteenth centuries and included many companies of professionally trained actors who performed elaborate plays depicting scenes of courtly and urban life.

As much as the corpus of scripts, the leading exponents also produced philosophical understandings of acting derived from their practical knowledge of theatre. Most well-known, the fourteenth-century court actor Zeami produced extensive treatises on and about theatre aesthetics (translated by Thomas Hare 2008). In addition to commentary on the chorus and musicality, these writings provide insights into the movement preparation of the actor, as well as the subtle attitudes required for an actor to attain the experience of *hana* (the flower), the sense of vital force. The detailed congruence between characters, movement and physical and mental preparation of theatre aesthetics correlates to Japanese philosophical and medical systems, as well as to ritual, calendrical and political values that circulated through the imperial courts from the Muromachi to the Tokugawa period (1333–1867).

As with Greek plays, Noh involves a limited number of leading actors – the *shite*, *waki* and *tsure*; as well as *kyogen* (comic actors who appear only in short interludes) – accompanied by a small chorus of singers and musicians. All performers train through repetitive instruction for many years, and undertake an apprenticeship in lesser roles, in order to realize the high performance standards of their art. An actor's skill lies in singing, dancing and other movements associated with portraying the character behind the mask: 'the actors "chants" (*utai*) and stylized "movements" (*mai*)' are not, according to Mae Smethurst, based on 'character expression in the Western sense of the word' (2013: 4). The chorus seems however to fulfil similar dramatic functions, such as commenting on the action between the main characters and drawing the audience into each scene with some critical distancing of the plot or translation of emotional registers in the drama. If we want to focus on how actors move on stage, then Zeami's elaborate descriptions of how a performer learns a role also reveal the philosophical concepts that imbue his teachings.

Zeami transcribed the manuscript, *Fushikaden*, 'The Art of the Flower', from his father's lessons to him and their company. In detailed, highly poetic, language, instructions are given for the imitation and representation of observable types within a broad repertory of plays. Given the theatre's proximity to the Japanese court, the talented actor must undertake close observation of the 'noblemen' who watch the performances and 'imitate down to the smallest detail the various things done by persons of high profession, especially those elements related to high artistic pursuits' (Zeami 1984: 10). The survival of the company involves pleasing the spectator, and so Zeami's father recommends against copying the 'vulgar'. Once the actor has observed and perfected the performance of type, 'through Effects and Attitudes', only later will they attend to what we might call performance presence, or being aware of being looked at.

Preparation of the actor begins through mastery of disciplined movement, such as the two key modes of sparring (in relatively mimetic movements) and dancing (Zeami 2008: 27). Sparring assists the agonistics of theatre, thus providing tactical knowledge of all types of conflict and contest between people and ideas, while the quality of dancing assists with communication of the lyrical, 'feminine' and poetic elements of the narrative. Different 'Styles of Movement' are indicated for more advanced character study so that in the 'Style of Intricate Movement', the physical technique involves 'stomping' in barefeet (a vigorous preparation that wakes up the body and vital organs) to connect the body to the experience of ground. As Zeami instructs more complex movements become overlaid with contrasting attitudes: 'move the body vigorously, stomp the feet with restraint; stomp the feet vigorously, move the body with restraint' (Zeami 2008: 145). Maintaining control of physical movement through the efforts of the will means that even a vigorous movement might still communicate 'with restraint' the sound or impression of the feet. This kind of paradoxical instruction differs considerably from the Western notion that in order to communicate particular emotional content, every action should be conducted with a singular intention.

Movement understandings which embrace such contradiction must be applied to the depiction of a demonic character – 'With form demonic, the intent is human' – whose threatening movements are also surreptitious and deviously human. Zeami suggests that a different kind of 'Violent Movement' would be necessary to depict a demon with a non-human heart, as a more monstrous figure, but cautions against using the 'momentary enthusiasm' of this style more than once (Zeami 2008: 146). That is, you can get excited about acting like a demon, stamping your feet and seeming wicked, but if this becomes a character type that you overly enlarge, then you will lose the subtle movements of the character. By realizing the nuance of affective attitudes through the different movement vocabulary associated with such characters, an actor will however learn to display 'energetic vitality' (131).

The key metaphor for an actor in this approach is that of 'the flower' (*hana*) which has different seasons and can at different times of day or night express different qualities:

> Giving your utmost to the repertory, finding a way to use your creativity, and understanding what creates the excitement of rarity; that's what the flower is. This is what I meant when I wrote: 'The flower is the mind, the seed, the techniques of performance.'
>
> (Zeami 2008: 65)

The flower represents the actor's energy, and their executing of learnt movements with 'a certain twist', that 'rarity', that will excite the unexpected in a performance. Imbued in Japanese aesthetics and design, the beauty of nature is what provides subtle inspiration for the actor's expressive power: the full blossom of spring, youthful and fresh, differs from the dark withered branches of winter in a sombre or mature interpretation. We might recall here Aristotle's observation that movement involves both withering and growth, in the sense that a living thing is not static even if in repose; it is always moving towards or away from some potentiality. For Zeami, the actor does not imitate the flower; rather, the actor understands the many states between generation and decay that will guide the actor to continue perfecting the art of performance. Too much movement will limit the audience's capacity to appreciate the circumstances that surround the representation – the wind, the light, the audience drinking too much, how a previous scene worked and how much energy should be used. With the sensibility of the flower, however, the expressive beauty of performance will transform into a poetic state of mind:

> An actor who has truly identified one aspect of the Flower, even though he has not mastered every form of Role Playing, may be able to grasp the beauty of Bending. Indeed, this quality can be said to exist at a stage even higher than that of the Flower. Without the Flower, Bending has no meaning. Without the Flower, the effect of Bending is merely gloomy and grey. The Bending of a Flower in full bloom is truly beautiful.
>
> (Zeami 1984: 28)

Awareness of the bending of their 'flower' may be applied to the professional career of a single actor, whose mutability of dramatic imitation will change over time, adapting rather than diminishing with age. Zeami's writings further expand on the 'imposing concept' of *yûgen*, variously translated as 'mystery, darkness and depth' or 'eroticism', that informs both plays and performance (Zeami 2008: 5):

> Although the text and the movements occupy separate concerns in the actor's mind, an actor who can make them reflect a single understanding should be considered an unsurpassed master. This makes for a truly strong performance. ... he is an actor who has naturally made the most of both strength and *yûgen*.
>
> (Zeami 2008: 188)

For the actor who aspires to achieve the 'wonder, excitement, intent, vision or voice' of *yûgen*, understanding the qualitative variations in movement from sparring to dancing, or flowering and wilting, becomes then both a spiritual and physical quest.

Contemporary actors who have participated in the rigorous, decades-long training practices of Japanese theatre will have experienced this profound mixture of intense physical training, stylized characters and the understanding of an elaborated theatre philosophy. Their theoretical texts articulate the desire for realization of the highest ideals of theatre aesthetics, a kind of transcendence, from dramatic imitation through movement into distinctive, yet mutable forms of poetic experience. Although highly codified, such methods are not static but continue to evolve, and such aspirations continue to inform a new generation of directors in Japan, such as Satoshi Miyagi, whose 2017 production of *Antigone* we will now discuss.

Case Study #1: *Antigone* (2017)

Miyagi's production follows a line of Japanese theatre directors, including Tadashi Suzuki, who have revisited classical Greek texts, animating their performances by embodying the grounding techniques and intense psychology of extant Japanese theatre traditions. The production that I saw at the Avignon Theatre Festival in 2017, a reworking of a production that premiered in Tokyo in 2004, was located in the Avignon Papal palace, against a three-sided backdrop of towering stonewalls; the audience was stacked on a scaffolding precipice of wooden benches. The sharp angular perspective heightened the dramatic lighting effects, which cast heavy shadows upon the rectangular pit of water that filled the stage below. The production began with the chorus, a large ensemble of actors dressed in silky white kimono and *oboshi* (trousers), touring the edge of the pool's wall, chanting and performing a gestural sequence in synchrony with their steps. In the first verses of the chorus, Sophocles hints that the people of Thebes might enjoy a 'night-long dance' to celebrate the end of a long war against Sparta, another city state; however, these actors of ambiguous identity – women, soldiers, servants, gravediggers and boatsmen – perform more modest rituals – flowing in and out of the action like the water that envelops the play as a whole.

Accompanied by *taiko* drumming and the strumming of the *koto*, and before any spoken words, the audience witnesses Creon's ceremonial burial of Eteocles, a ritual prepared with libations in glass globes and a wooden burial stick. What are the chorus at this time? Perhaps priests whose slow gestural movements suggest the presence of spirit beings, or gods, rather than a recognizable social world, and the eeriness continues when the two sisters Antigone and Ismene, performed by celebrity pop singers, appear wearing shiny white wigs and talking with high-pitched voices. Strewn across a series of rocky islands, both Antigone and Ismene cling to the sharp ledges as they argue, and their awkward positioning is contrasted with the chorus who sways and hovers around them. With boats, some members of the chorus row Creon to Antigone's hiding place and then transport Antigone to the corpse of Polynices for her own solemn ritual.

Although Sophocles's drama builds from the tension and pain of Antigone outwards through the confrontation with Creon, in this Japanese production the chorus has an all-pervasive effect; the choral formation in the water and surrounding the action reverberates between the ritual, role and duty investigated by the play. But their rhythmic walking movements also produce an atmosphere of tremulous uncertainty. With Antigone imprisoned and Creon's wrath overflowing, they sing a lament:

Fortunate they whose lives have no taste of pain. For those whose house is shaken by the gods, escape no kind of doom. It extends to all the kin like the wave that comes when the winds of Thrace run over the dark of the sea. The black sand of the bottom is brought from the depths; the beaten capes sound back with a hollow cry.

(Sophocles 1959: 180)

Miyagi's watery setting is not merely theatrical effect but a considered response to the pain that is carried in the winds and dark waters of the play. Without the movement of the chorus as the medium – their consistent attentiveness contrasting with the unreconciled speech – there would be no tragedy, and without the contrasting nature of water and rocks, impermanent and permanent, especially in the absence of direct translation (Greek to Japanese, with French surtitles but no English), the doom of the broken funeral rituals would make little sense. When the time comes to drown the bodies of Antigone and Haemon, the ashen, white figures of the chorus step into the water, soaking their garments, ebbing and flowing as if with the outgoing tide. After the final speech, the exode, a slow procession of these white ghosts around the rectangular wall commences again; some performers were drenched and their garments sticky, while the wind blew at the edges of other sleeves. Time passed, until the last actor gathered himself from the boat back into the unifying chorus, spiralling back from duty into the assembled rhythm. Caught in this movement pulse, the audience, of which I was part, was left with a profound sense of soulful loss – as if we felt the 'anima' departing.

I think this production raises an important question: how do we stage the chorus in the twenty-first century? Is there a way to return that experience of 'rhythm expressed in motion' to the vicissitudes of tragedy? It could be argued that Miyagi's theatre with its ritualizing of spectacle placates a society somewhat numbed to the psychological limits of human power and hubris. And yes, by drawing the spectators into a mesmerizing liminality of cathartic movement, the images felt like we were all cleansed in the watery abyss below. Debates about this production suggested that it offered a Japanese perspective on justice systems administered with little thought of the human consequences, hence the stark use of natural elements – water and rocks – in play with dramaturgy of discord. And being imprisoned on an island or cast adrift are evocative movement metaphors of alienation. To my mind, the chorus formations certainly contributed to the *yûgen*, or solemn mystery, of its ancient harmonies, as well as the jarring sense of a contemporary supernatural meaning. The chorus might indeed be one of the ways in which theatre of the twenty-first century can assemble the qualities of rhythm that Lefebvre proposed in the Introduction, by reconnecting the individual to the social, and the social to the cyclical rhythms of the organic world.

Miyagi's reputation as a director resides, then, in these formal aesthetics as well as his fine attunement to theatre and its political and social conditions (Smethurst 2011). Restaging *Antigone* for Avignon in 2017, Miyagi's representation of the drowning chorus, managing the transition towards death across the Styx, provides a contemporary commentary on rising sea levels and the failure of governments to respond to climate change. Such images also cause reflection on the Fukushima nuclear disaster in which Japanese citizens were not allowed to bury their dead after the subsequent tsunami and poisoning of the landscape. In the court of honour of the Avignon palace, all the drifting white bodies of contemporary injustice could become then our own versions of a ghostly chorus.

For Plato, the serious intent of the chorus requires 'both acute perception and understanding of rhythms and harmoniai' as well as moral authority, while for Aristotle, rhythm and harmonies could have many purposes, including aesthetic appreciation (Plato 2014: 93). Contemporary directors – not only Miyagi but also Western artists such as Robert Wilson and Anne Bogart – create the poly-rhythms of chorality by instilling the discipline of metre in the theatre ensemble and in doing so, they also examine relations between 'natural' harmonies and *yûgen* in order to excavate the power of ritualized responses to communal events in the world today.

Gesture: Roman rhetoric

Returning to the second and first century BCE, it is possible to attend more closely to movement arising from the actor and situation in Western secular traditions of theatre. The Roman development of the specialist role of actors, as we shall see, is another reminder of how theatre techniques shape bodily attitudes and expression. C. W. Marshall's *The Stagecraft and Performance of Roman Comedy* (2006) offers many insights into how movement was mobilized by the masks and routines of stage space in the plays of Roman playwrights such as Plautus and Terence. As with Greek drama, a strong sense of rhythmic metre governed dramatic speech, and music, particularly the pipe, interacted with the spoken word. Building on popular mime troupes and Greek dramatic models, these Roman comedies also give credence to the role of character types in masked pantomimes that carefully shape dramatic expectations. Comedic form, for instance, highlights the necessity of managing stage movement and shows how an actor's improvisation could be expected to focus and engage the audience's attention.

Marshall usefully theorizes two other features of stage movement. The first is structural, that of the use of doors for entrances and exits; and the second is the continuity of stage action. Indicative entrances and exits in Roman stage architecture, according to Marshall, were also symbolic: stage left faced the urban centre of town, while stage right led to the harbour or countryside, and, indeed, Roman scripts established conventions of 'stage left and right' as specific directions towards town or harbour and countryside (Marshall 2006: 50). These conventions towards the offstage world were enhanced by three doors at the rear of the stage which allowed comic plots to have different characters enter or exit. In the *Bacchides* (likely an adaptation from the Greek) by Titus Maccius Plautus, for instance, one door leads to the house of a citizen, another to a temple and the third to the brothel or slave's house. Rapid movement interaction in the short space between the doors can facilitate a great variety of street scenes and character changes, but it is easy to imagine how mistaken entries or discovered departures from one door or another – visiting the prostitute instead of the church, for instance – might lead to comic mishap.

'Pace', which is the speed with which actions accumulate and are distributed across the work, according to Marshall, was also critical to Roman performance (2006: 174–7). Pace does not imply rushing through speech or action; rather, the metre of speech, divisions within the structure of the plot and the architecture of the stage combine to score the type and quality of movement. Recent translations of Roman plays often include the division into 'acts' and place stage instructions at the periphery of the spoken dialogue to indicate the familiar device of continuous movement – as one set of characters leaves, another comes in. While brief moments of 'emptying' may suggest time passing, the audience perceives both real time and imaginative time, shifting between one set of actions and another to a different time and place, thus rendering theatre movement as disjunctive and episodic. Given this movement transition between one place and another, a crucial aspect of 'empty time' becomes the number of beats that elapse between scenes. This Roman stage convention can exaggerate the effects of a different 'realistic' stage world in relation to the previous scene. Hence, a comedic effect that highlights the absurdity of a situation might involve a swift cut between characters exposed in different scenarios, a movement device frequently observed today in stand-up routines or television comedies. And, as the Roman educator and lawyer Quintillian suggests, each production was shaped by the specific attributes and physicality of the actors and their skills in improvisation. To summarize, this combination of Roman rhetorical persuasion and the conventions of comic form offer various theories of movement to shape a repertoire of gesture, improvised timing and the manipulation of stage relations between on- and offstage worlds.

If Roman plays flexibly adapted Greek theatrical content and ideas to the entertainment needs of Roman imperial rule and its desire for spectacle, Quintilian theorized rhetoric by explaining how gesture can communicate attitudes to an audience. His twelve volumes on *The Institutes of Oratory* were written in 95 AD (approximately one to two hundred years after plays by Plautus and Terence) and eloquently draw upon the theatre to present rules of movement, comportment and expression for civic speech. Concerned with the power of oratory to communicate, he realizes that 'if gesture and the expression of the face are out of harmony with the speech, if we look cheerful when our words are sad, or shake our heads when making a positive assertion, our words will not only lack weight, but will fail to carry conviction. Gesture and movement are also productive of grace' (Quintillian 2001: 119).

In the Western tradition, Quintilian formulates interest in the nuances of bodily movement, by asking how does a gesture carry meaning as well as appeal to the emotions 'without the help of words'? He understands thought can be communicated kinetically with a 'power' that may 'seem more powerful than speech itself' (2001: 119). Gestural expression, as he elaborates, can punctuate and reinforce the meaning of a speech, but it can also be superfluous and perhaps confusing. Noting that the 'grace' of 'gesture and movement' can only be acquired through practice, he introduces the example of an actor: 'This is why Demosthenes used to plan his performance in front of a big mirror; despite the fact that the bright surface reverses the image, he had complete trust in his own eyes' ability to tell him what effect he was making' (2001: 21). Even two thousand years ago, Demosthenes practising his lines was adapting his gestural movements and general comportment to make a better impression.

Quintilian also elaborates on the appropriate gestures encoded for certain kinds of idea, event or expression, whether it be for emphasis in a criminal trial, to draw attention to the orator's digressions and elaborations, or to bring to mind something for the listener that may be at the periphery of their vision or understanding. He suggests that walking, stepping back and hand-waving can be useful but should not be florid or 'effeminate'. Excessive use of movement tricks to captivate the spectator or a caricature of gestures imitating particular social classes is also to be avoided. In a sense his instructions serve as one of the first acting manuals because it is not in 'nature' for the orator to harness the full repertoire of expression but they can be 'assisted by study' towards perfection of physical attributes. 'Stage actors' are, not surprisingly, figures of comparison for Quintilian since they 'add so much to the greatest poets' (2001: 87). In the following passage, he illuminates how two 'great comic actors' make use of their physically distinct attributes:

> Demetrius and Stratocles, give pleasure by ... the peculiar, and non-transferable features of each. The hand-waving, the lovely long cries meant for the audience, the way of catching the wind in his clothes as he came on, the occasional expressive movement of his right side – all this became Demetrius and no one else; his height and his good looks helped him in it all. What became Stratocles, on the other hand, was his speed and agility, his laugh (not always in keeping with the character but a conscious concession to the audience), and even his hunched-up neck. If the other had done any of these things, it would have seemed a disgusting performance.
>
> (Quintilian 2001: 179–81)

Connecting an actor's delivery to that feeling of what 'should become us well' rather than general rules leads, he suggests, to artistic accomplishment and audience praise (2001: 88). Quintilian's guidance on rhetoric also portrays the conviction of the consummate political leader or the eloquence of a magistrate in a court setting. Think of theatrical examples where a famous speech is required, perhaps Portia in the *Merchant of Venice* or Galileo defending himself in Brecht's play of that name. It will be the artful combinations of gesture and physicality, rhetoric and persuasion, that convinces the listener of the speech's truth or validity. The performative art of rhetoric is, as Mauss suggested, an acquired technique of the body but as Quintilian's text instructs, it can also be deceptive. The following case study of Douglas Wright's *I Am My Own Wife* provides a recent political context through which to reflect upon the role of the actor's rhetorical agency and gestural fluidity in the fabrication of a fictional identity.

Case Study #2: *I Am My Own Wife* (2003)

In a clever piece of verbatim theatre, Wright tells the story of Charlotte von Mahlsdorf, an East German transgender woman who lives an ambiguous identity as an antiquarian shop owner before, during and after the Second World War and Cold War. Having killed her father and spent time in prison, her home becomes a refuge, housing the antique museum and basement cabaret bar from which she earns a living, albeit partially illicit. With these multiple secrets, perhaps spying for the Stasi, she masks her identity from the Nazis, then the communists and prying neighbours.

Based on von Mahlsdorf's autobiography, the first Broadway production in 2003 was a lengthy collaboration between the writer, the director Moisés Kaufman and solo actor Jefferson Mays. Charlotte is dressed throughout in 'a simple black housedress with peasant stitching, a kerchief on her head, and an elegant strand of pearls', so the performance demands a continuous shifting of rhetorical registers to reveal the multiple characters inhabiting the narrative (Wright 2004: 5). These include von Mahlsdorf – young and old, male and female; the playwright and the journalist who first documents her story; and nearly thirty other characters such as German soldiers, jailors and neighbours or museum visitors.

With minimalist costume changes, such as putting on a cap or removing the scarf, the actor's speech must be accompanied by subtle changes in comportment – leaning forward, standing upright – and a detailed movement repertoire – turns of the head, squinting of the eyes, fumbling of the hands – that befits each character incarnation. The opening lines are indicative of the curiosity she engenders: 'She gazes at the audience for a moment; the tiniest flicker of a smile dances on her lips. Then, surprisingly, she closes the doors as quickly as she appeared, and is gone' (Wright 2004: 6). Her primary prop is an old phonograph, which allows the actor to deflect attention to the music while the pearls function like worry-beads dramatizing her anxiously constructed refinement. Quintilian observes that without the hands, all delivery 'would be crippled and enfeebled', as he explains:

> Other parts of the body assist the speaker: the hands, I might almost say, speak for themselves. Do we not use them to demand and promise, summon and dismiss, threaten and beg, show horror and fear, inquire and deny, and also to indicate joy, sadness, doubt, confession, remorse, or again size, quantity, number and time? Do they not excite, recite, restrain, approve, admire, display shame? Do they not serve instead of adverbs and pronouns when we need to point out places or persons? Amid all the linguistic diversity of the peoples and nations of the world, this, it seems to me, is the common language.
>
> (2001: 129)

Even if there is not a 'common language' of the hands, Mays used his hands descriptively and busily, as did the Australian actor Ben Gerrard that I saw perform this role in 2017. As male hands, they hold an axe and move furniture, but as female hands they fretfully wipe themselves on the black apron. There are also the 'effeminate' hands that hold up antique objects to explain their provenance to the audience. With her fingers stroking, the actor brings von Mahlsdorf, the museum curator, to life by speaking with tenderness about those things – the furniture, music boxes and mirrors – that have contained and filled her life.

Looking like a mime with black costume and white hands, the hands also ensure 'physical eloquence' so that, as Quintillian asserts, 'if the Delivery is changed, the same words can suggest, affirm, reproach, deny, wonder, show indignation, ask a question, mock or disparage' (Quintilian 2001: 177). A gesture therefore is always performative, it can punctuate speech, but it can also deflect and interfere with meaning. When von Mahlsdorf rails against the state, the actor's delivery is loud, square-footed and blunt, but she must also charm, and show wonder, to strange visitors who knock at the door of her East German apartment.

Quintilian's lessons about the orator's gestures take on an embodied life as a double lexicon for this remarkable character: 'No matter what people want to see or hear, I'll show or play it. Some people, they come to see me. *Ich bin Transvestit.* But soon they look at the furniture' (Wright 2004: 14). She plays against nature, defying the singularity of what Judith Butler has called the performativity of gender identity, 'manufactured through a sustained set of acts, posited through the gendered stylization of the body' (Butler 2006: xv). Butler famously argues that the gendered body becomes inscribed by the regulatory fictions required by normative codes and behaviours and that there can be violent consequences of not conforming to either masculine or feminine bodily codes (2006: xx). Von Mahlsdorf seems to have realized that regime change and punitive laws surrounding her desires would need to be hidden by the fiction of a fluent gestural vocabulary. Watching the production, the rapid flourishes of Mays's hands certainly distract the audience from the ambiguous signs of the flat chest and the hardening lines of his face. The gestures become the visible signs of the convincing speech act; for surely, the ultimate rhetorical claim of dissembling with gender, career and personal history is to persuade us of von Mahlsdorf's survival through decades of surveillance, imprisonment and discrimination.

Style: the *Natyasastra*

Before departing from classical movement theories, I want to turn to another non-Western treatise on theatre, which, in its level of detail and specificity, extends far beyond the texts of Aristotle and Quintilian. I am referring here to the *Nāṭya Śāstra* (*Natyasastra*, pronounced Natyashastra), compiled over several centuries to 200 BCE, and although most likely a syncretic text, it is attributed to the Indian philosopher Bharata Muni. This immense volume of writings on 'Hindu dramaturgy and histrionics' includes thirty-six chapters on all aspects of the performing arts from the structure of texts, stage architecture, specific dances and the use of gestures to convey specific emotional states, as well as the conditions of audience pleasure. Like other philosophers, the sage Bharata identifies theatre as a powerful medium and writes in dialogue with those he instructs:

> The drama ... is a mimicry of actions and conducts of people, which is rich in various emotions and which depicts different situations. This will relate to actions of men good, bad and indifferent, and will give courage, amusement and happiness as well as counsel to them all ... There is no wise maxim, no learning, no art or craft, no device, no action that is not found in the drama.
>
> (Ghosh 1950: 108)

Elaborating the 'States and Sentiments' of drama, this aesthetic theory reflects not only upon the attributes of an artist's performance of theatre and poetry but extends to theatre's role as moral and spiritual guidance. When Indian philosopher Abhinavagupta in the tenth century adds to the *Natyasastra*, he stresses reception, with his concept of *rasa* (often translated as 'taste') offered to assess the sublime appreciation of poetry. Two notable differences from Western theatre theory are, first, that women were never excluded from the stage as they are in Western stagecraft by moral codes, or masculine civic and religious authorities, and, secondly, dance, music and the visual arts retained a vital role in the presentation and understanding of theatre. What is remarkable is that this Hindu philosophy has flourished for centuries so that even today, when many of its ideas about gender, caste and human conduct are outdated, many of the principles and teachings about embodied practice are still influential in Indian performance genres. Hence they offer alternative theories of movement and theatre.

In the *Natyasastra*, all Hindu plays are referred to as drama; however, they would have been more akin to genres such as opera, ballet or musical theatre, and rather than be divided into comedies and tragedies with distinctive narrative arcs, they represent four different 'styles' of presentation: 'the Verbal, the Grand, the Energetic, and the Graceful'. Each style has its own preponderance of modes of speech, gestural delivery and characterizations defined by movement, that in turn give shape to different types of 'sentiments' or *rasa*, although there are some overlaps: the Verbal elicits the Pathetic and Marvellous; the Grand elicits the Heroic, the Marvellous and the Furious; the Energetic applies to the Terrible, the Odious and the Furious; while Graceful and modulated speech is proper to 'the Erotic and Comic Sentiments' (Ghosh 1950: LXI). A particular drama will include combinations of these sentiments, and thus styles of performance vary in the extent to which they depend on spoken or physical skills, interaction with music, and elaborate or visually specific costumes.

As with Aristotle's division of theatre into segments that differentiate between movements of the chorus and those which progress the narrative, the *Natyasastra* delineates a sequence of scenes, including Preliminaries, Blessings and Laudation. It further identifies ten kinds of play, divided into acts with five kinds of plot junctures – opening, progression, development, pause and conclusion. It includes detailed prescriptions for the use of costume and make-up, for the varieties of metre (rhythmic patterning), and for the representation of character types – the portrayal of 'the woman of swine-type' or 'of horse-type' – and outlines appropriate interactions between characters, such as the 'King's etiquette towards women', 'Signs of a maiden's love' or 'Declamations of old people' (Ghosh 1950: XXXI). Every facet of drama is so densely delineated that an expert artist takes years to master the requisite skills. The *Natyasastra* is a vivid reminder that preparation of an actor – involving the intricacies of movement expression – must become deeply embodied and situated within a repertoire of performance works.

The emphasis on spectacle (seemingly decried by Aristotle) is given full imaginative rein in the *Natyasastra*. Theatre should delight in the performative aspects of display, such as the use of colour in make-up, or stylized injunctions for comportment and gesture, and it conceptualizes how rhythmic movements relate to four forms of corporeal representation (*abhinaya*), such as *angika, vacika, aharya* and *sattvika*. In the section explaining *angika*, the expression of the limbs, various gestures and postures are given precise significance.

> [T]he head has thirteen different gestures which are as follows: *Akampita*: Moving the head slowly up and down. *Kampita*: when the movements in the *Akampita* head are quick and copious. (Uses): The *Akampita* head is to be applied in giving a hint, teaching questioning, addressing in an ordinary way (lit. naturally) and giving an order. The *Kampita* head is applicable (lit. desired) in anger, argument, understanding, asserting, threatening, sickness and intolerance.
>
> (Ghosh 1950: 150)

And so it continues with the articulation of each body part given a qualitative dimension so that, as with the example of moving the head up and down slowly, any movement of limbs or face must be carefully practised in relation to particular characters or attitudes. Gestures of the head, according to the translator Ghosh, can be either realistic, within ordinary or everyday life (with naturalism in the acting), or theatrical, using stylized and rhythmic gestures to incorporate other actions in the manner of dance patterns. Another style, *Angahara*, explicitly includes dance figures, and *karanas*, which may be either major or minor for the 'movement of limbs' (Ghosh 1950: 45). Repetition and movement articulation in theatrical codes are acquired and then drawn upon to build a dramatic performance with recognizable characters and narrative elements. While Hindu theatre has its own tradition of plays and festival events to support dramatic cycles of entertainment, the forms distilled in the expertise of the Natyasastra are also used in more contemporary manifestations of polyrhythmic and polymorphic expression. Reproduction of the detailed encoding of types expected of the classical Indian actor might be rejected today, but the following case study explores how a practice of gestural specificity, aligned with strict tempo, may adapt and improvise with ideas from the *Natyasastra*.

Case Study #3: *Zero Degrees* (2005)

The multi-media performance of *Zero Degrees* (2005) involved collaboration between British-Bengali dancer Akram Khan, Belgian choreographer-dancer Sidi Larbi Cherkaoui, composer Nitin Sawnhey and sculptor Anthony Gormley. Both Khan and Sawnhey, the children of South Asian immigrants, studied Indian classical art forms such as the dance genre, *kathak* (Khan) and the *tabla* drum (Sawnhey) during childhood. Requiring years of training, both forms have strongly metrical components that have inspired theoretical mathematicians, as well as artists from the Beatles's George Harrison in the song 'Norwegian Wood' to the contemporary *kathak* 'Desi' hip-hop. In the embodiment of *kathak*, there are rigorous expectations for the live accompaniment of physical movement with music and narrative. As British-Indian dance scholar Royona Mitra explains: 'Complex footwork of mathematical precision known as *tatkar*, extreme speed in motion, and controlled and successive pirouettes of the torso called *chakkars*, are characteristic features of *kathak*' (2015: 8). The counting metre extends from a 16 beat cycle to repeats of 64, and my sense from the dancers' faces is of them concentrating silently as they shuttle through the complex rhythmic cycles. The rhythmic pounding of the feet contrasts with the expressive and circular use of the *angika* or upper body gestures which narrate the stories. Coordinating footwork with gestures and the capacity of *abhinaya*, or facial expression, to convey moods and emotions means that *kathak* performers have virtuosic movement abilities.

The *Zero Degrees* dramaturgy is structured as a series of vignettes between Khan and Cherkaoui that examine contemporary issues of diasporic migration and displacement. In one early scene, the two dancers sit side by side recounting in unison the story of events taking place at a border checkpoint. Punctuated precisely with a syllabic metre, perhaps 'made up of four feet which expresses different ideas and consists of short and long syllables', they stress each word carefully (Ghosh 1950: 256). Utterance then, as the Natyasastra emphasizes, includes making pattern from metre: 'there is no word, without rhythm and no rhythm, without words' (Ghosh 1950: 256). Each word is demonstrated by a series of hand gestures that illustrate the story in a stylized manner. A sweep of the hands to one side, for instance, follows the smooth movement of the red European passport through a mass of green Pakistani passports held high, or the drawing together of two fingers indicates the gaze of an anxious relative watching and waiting at the border. The tension in the hands and the rapid flow of actions in the story circumscribe what the Natyasastra describes of the 'Sentiments', felt by Khan, 'the Pathetic and the Marvellous', as he realizes the power of his own passport to override the local travellers. Inhabiting what Mitra calls 'the "third space" of border identity politics', Khan is both a Bangladeshi and an outsider, and the synchronous narration through gesture evokes the frequent discomfort of being a transnational subject moving between countries (2015: 101). Shifts between storytelling and abstract movement are a feature of much Indian theatre, and this scene concludes with the two artists side by side, adopting a rhythmic pattern that bounces back and forth: swinging their arms in a crossing motion across their chests, and while maintaining the same beat, slowly falling out of time. The erratic metre, perhaps representing disharmony, replicates the demanding repetitions of travel, and the contrast between the wheels clicking on a train track and the stress, tedium and displacement allows the impact of the story – its *rasa* – to be absorbed by the audience.

The relentless counting of the drum overlaid by the sinuous sounds of the sitar also gives a propulsive dynamics to the performance: 'The energy of their movement exchanges ranges from mutuality, to fragility, to coercion, to control, to manipulation, to volatility, to acceptance as they explode into the whole space' (Mitra 2015: 100). And it is hard to imagine another theatre genre in which corporeal rhythm is so explicitly determining. When a form of contest emerges between the virtuosity of Khan and Cherkaoui, they spin, slap, bounce, criss-cross and fall against the floor and each other, absorbing each challenge but making the rhythmic responses into a voluble sign language. In another example, the two life-sized mannequins, or 'dummies', created by Gormley that share the stage with the dancers move from being powerful objects, 'commenting' by observing and being observed, to surrogates of the lifeless self. When Cherkaoui gets his dummy to pat the other dummy on the head – raising and lowering a hand, both realistic and stylized movement – it is amusing, but when he then continues with the same action to beat the dummy into the floor, the habitual gesture gives form to the cold detachment of violent repression.

In *Zero Degrees*, the performers do not become characters; however, the rapid fire physical vocabulary, the metric modulations of the score, and the abstract codes for relating body and dummy seem dependent upon the ancient knowledges that the *Natyasastra* teaches, in which a stylized gesture may be attached to both a sign and a sentiment in the service of drama. For the contemporary artist Khan, negotiating subject positions that exist in-between states of identity, the 'powerful and phenomenological medium' of precise movement produces a theatre which evokes 'solace, comfort and escapism' as well as offering a powerful critique of border politics (Mitra 2015: 105).

Appreciating the multi-layered complexity of the *Natyasastra* and its contribution to aesthetic theory cannot be accomplished here but, as I suggested earlier, many of its ideas continue in forms of classical Indian dance, such as Bharatanatyam, and musical *ragas* practised today. A similar continuity of stylized and metrical performance with precise gestural vocabularies exists in many other folk forms, and some of these movement repertoires have migrated into popular performance genres of Bollywood musicals and hip-hop. In dance and popular culture, a connection therefore between stylized theatrical expression and rhythmic movement, with its power to illustrate or amplify 'sentiment', seems obvious – it can turn up the heat, making the audience marvel, or keep them cool in the face of the 'odious' – so the reasons for the separation between elaborate movement stylization and Western theatre are worth considering in the following discussion of medieval theatre.

Processions: medieval theatre

If movement theories are embodied in social and theatrical practices, how does the theatre adapt its movement genres and techniques when geopolitical horizons change or temporal breaks occur in a particular way of life? After the Roman celebration of comedies, circuses and other ludic activities, and the sophisticated codification of oratory, the collapse of the Roman Empire led to a relative decline in the efficacy of large-scale, theatrical conventions. A growing division between secular and religious life in the regulation of the public sphere, and a loss of designated theatre venues, also led to greater suspicion about performance arts. Characterized as the Western Middle Ages, this period also saw distinctions between literary culture and non-literary culture widen and reinforce religious, pagan and secular cultures. Unless sanctioned by the church, public performances were condemned and troupes of mummers (actors), roving musicians and dancers were considered threatening to the symbolic universe of Christian theology. Yet vital signs of movement were everywhere: in itinerant wanderings; in religious iconography and in diverse folk practices, whether as street entertainments, ritualized jousting or festive gatherings.

Where extant philosophy from the medieval period refers back to the 'ancients', it upholds the lofty ideals of a rarefied tragic sphere onto which authors project a Christian universe of reason and divine order. In terms of theory, text and word is privileged so that religious oratory dominates over spoken dialogue, justification replaces sensation and soul (or mind) redeems the body. In spite of this idealization of human existence in terms of religious conduct, the evidence of vibrant social practices have generated movement theories. First, the religious dances of death, such as the *danses macabres*, represent bleak, if terrifying, escapes from the sentence of everyday life rituals across a wide range of media (Oosterwijk and Knöll 2011). Secondly, the concept of *choreomania* (commonly called St Vitus's dance) became regarded as a 'convulsive epidemic' although it may have been a register of the 'unruly movement of crowds' in medieval society (Gotman 2018). And thirdly, processionals become a powerful genre of theatrical movement, often associated with the staging of medieval mystery plays, and widely representative of displays of power. This weird combination of suspicion and stress, with affirmation and glory, determines many facets of ceremonial movement as well as the social hierarchies of the procession.

Inherited from pagan ceremonies of blessing the fields, religious processions involve dedicated groups walking together and following a formal progression between sites. For the Romans the processional was a performance of triumph after a battle victory, when they could display captured slaves, goods and animals. Later, inventing a Christian tradition, Pope Gregory gave a famous sermon, the *Letania Septiformis*, that marks the transition from Roman Christianity to the Christianity of the sixth century CE (Latham 2015: 25).

Notably the Pope's proclamation outlined the form and purposes of processional liturgy – dramatic points of departure from the church doors, a vast cast and progressive prayers with specified actions by the priests – and this genre over centuries amplified the power of the church against catastrophe. Especially on rogation days and at the feast of Corpus Christi, processions and pilgrimages to cult sites were arranged that could combine medieval superstition with the public rituals of a fervent religious mysticism.

Outside theatre, processionals remained a feature of much other religious and secular drama, and festival parades were and still are always popular with a crowd. The Persian theatrical genre of *taziyeh* dramatizes, for instance, a religious narrative depicting the tragic martyrdom of a much-loved Imam, and endures in diverse formats, including staged drama, in many countries of the Near East. One account describes a series of episodes that travel: 'a race around the *sakku* by armed horsemen symbolizes a battle, a person turning around himself means a change of place or character; a large basin of water represents the river Euphrates and straw plays the role of desert sand' (Rubin et al. 2001: 195). Embodying symbolic actions and places, this ancient history of the processional format has been maintained to stir emotional and collective memory even as it also underscores present political realities (Ristvit 2015).

Theatre scholar Dieter Mehl argues that religious processions have had a lengthy influence on theatre so that in medieval Europe the 'Corpus Christi processions in the larger towns' functioned as symbolic dramas orchestrated to include 'magnificent pageants, interspersed with pantomimes and tableaux vivants' (1965: 7). They were also perhaps tragic affairs such as the bleak scene of penitent processionals seen in the 1956 film, *The Seventh Seal*, directed by Ingmar Bergman. Shot in black and white, the film depicts a procession of flagellants – a line of half-naked men lashing one another; monks struggling under the weight of huge crosses or with aching arms holding skulls over their bowed heads; and the faces of children who wear the pain of poverty, sickness and bitterness. However, the narrative also follows the antics of a group of itinerant comedians whose folk entertainments are only temporarily interrupted by the procession. Such contradictions in theatrical movement coincide with Mehl's argument that the mobile, comically subversive and improvised elements from medieval processions filtered into the mimed 'dumb shows' that led to the rise of theatre in Elizabethan cities. Such pantomime entertainments could serve a number of dramatic functions, such as allowing unscripted movements to parody elements of courtly life or 'playing by signs' those serious dramatic events, such as murders and funerals, that cannot be described verbally (Mehl 1965: 4).

On a more celebratory note, it is easy to be swept away by the pageantry of court processionals. The German drama, *Otto of Wittelsbach, or the Choleric Count* (1801), gives us a vivid account of the grandeur of royal hierarchies:

> The procession appears. Fifty guards pass through the gallery, followed by many Knights and Nobles magnificently clothed. In the midst of them walks the Duke, supported by Egbert and another Peer. Henry joins them. After the Duke, walks the Duchess, supported by two ladies of rank, and followed by others. These are succeeded by more Knights and Nobles, and fifty guards close the procession.
>
> (Babo 1801: 7)

Such civic display highlights key features of processional movement: linear, orderly and rhythmically scored, this figuration includes the hierarchical scale and positioning of horizontal and vertical, while the velocity of appearance and disappearance can have a mesmerizing effect on the spectator, as anyone who has watched a street parade or cavalcade of passing dignitaries will attest.

Modern dramatists, such as Friedrich Dürrenmatt in *The Visit* (1956), use these features of the procession as a recognizable movement genre. The narrative recounts the long-awaited return of village woman, Claire Zachanassian, who has become extraordinarily wealthy in a distant urban life, and the play begins with a preparation for 'some procession' that turns into 'interminable processions', repeatedly stalled and interrupted, that are watched by the Mayor, the Pastor and the Teacher, along with an excited and restless crowd from the village (Dürrenmatt 1973: 11, 24). Porters enter carrying 'an endless stream of cases and trunks' and stumble forward, inviting the spectator to imagine each item of luggage as the rich and ceremonial spoils of Zachanassian's history of achievement, exploitation, consumption and reward (Dürrenmatt 1973: 24). Carried into the town square on a sedan chair, she rides above the pitiful comedy below, which is littered with reminders of the poor and infirm just like a Corpus Christi procession but also recalling the beaten bodies of post-war European towns rendered as penitents to American efforts at 'reconstruction'. Men stand on a bench pretending to be trees, and the Butler leads two blind men by the hand as Claire steps from the sedan. The image of the villagers celebrating her return as salvation of their destitute existence is grotesquely overturned when they fail to accede to Claire's demand to have her former lover killed. This contemporary 'morality play', re-imagined by Dürrenmatt through processional movement, contradicts then the religious values of Christian redemption after wrongdoing, as well as mocking a capitalism that pretends to a future of benign generosity.

In theatre and performance studies, I regard the procession as a significant movement genre. One individual or group following another produces a social formation that assembles bodies into an embodied transitive structure: it can reinforce religious belief or reveal the pomp of wealth or power, but it also signifies the ordinary struggle of journeying from birth to death. What is the theory here? One in which moving from sacred rite to sacred site becomes a collective movement that controls and shapes excess public emotion. It may unleash tears, prayers or wailing to ensure supplication, or perhaps its opposite, admit a buffoonery and comic relief as a participatory rebellion against the solemn authority of church or state.

The visual artist William Kentridge with his film installation, *Shadow Procession* (1999), set in the post-apartheid era of South Africa provides a contemporary example of the ways in which processions can suture together the secular and the religious, history and the body. Masked by rules about conduct and service, processional formats make mass movement visible and hence give theatrical shape to affects that extend beyond individual expression to the play of power in mobilizing social groups across borders of morality, ideology and geography. We could think here of the Global Climate Strike, with the mass demonstration of school children marching with their banners, placards and messages for the world's leaders.

Anti-theatrical hostility: moral censorship

In the Renaissance theatre of Europe, the condemnation of movement by the church had an enduring impact on theatre history, both as 'anti-theatrical prejudice' and the separation of dance from theatre. Before the rich flourishing of theatre in the Elizabethan period, references to sixteenth-century theatre theory usually include Stephen Gosson's 'Anatomy of Abuses', which railed against the infamy and degradation of British morals in popular entertainments. Another strident attack came from preacher John Northbrooke, whose *Treatise against Dicing, Dancing, Plays, and Interludes, with Other Idle Pastimes* (1577) condemned actors as 'loitering, idle persons' along with 'ruffians, blasphemers, and swinge bucklers, so many drunkards, tosspots, whoremasters, dauncers, fiddlers, and minstrels, diceplayers and maskers, fencers, thieves, interlude players, cutpurses, cosiners, masterless servants, jugglers, rogues, sturdy beggars (and) counterfaite Egyptians' (Northbrooke 1843: 76). Pretty much everyone in this assorted company was regarded as corrupting and potentially the work of the devil.

Participation in the playful movement of theatre became dangerously associated with the 'becks and gestures of the body', that might, Northbrooke acknowledges, be 'expressing their meaning and thoughts' (1843: 50). Supporting his argument with classical and biblical references, Northbrooke admits that orchestrated movement may have diverse origins, including observation of 'the sundry motions of wandering stars' and that there could therefore be legitimate and illegitimate reasons for dancing:

> There is also another kinde of dauncing, whereby men were exercised in warrelike affayres, for they were commaunded to make gestures, and to leape, hauing vpon them their armour, for that afterwarde they might be the more prompt to fight, when neede (for the publike weale) should require ... There is another kynde of dauncing, which was instituted onely for pleasure and wantonnesse sake: this kynde of daunces Demetricus Cynicus derided, calling it a thing vayne, and nothing worth. And, if you speake onely of this kynde of daunce, I say, as he sayth, it is vaine, foolish, fleshly, filthie, and diuelishe.
>
> (1843: 145)

Hence, dancing for serious joy or military action is permitted, whereas pleasurable and wanton movements are condemned. In terms of movement theory, Northbrooke however recognizes that movement can 'make gestures' that signify the 'fleshly' of a body's thinking and that dancing may contribute to a cosmological experience of the world. The problem for Northbrooke is that the unruly dances – 'hoppings and leapings' – of the Elizabethan populace involve too much 'intermingling' (1843: 150). Moreover 'carnal pleasure' from movement might undermine respectful worship, and so the corrupting effects of the stage must be prohibited. These views also have an ontological dimension, which sees the mutability of theatrical representation as threatening to the religious view of a stable universe created by God. If an actor can be duplicitous in performance, or a man can dress as a woman, this freedom of imagination disturbs hierarchical and gendered morality, for as Gosson argued 'the minde must be simple without mingle mangle of fish and flesh, good and bad' (cited in Barish 1981: 89).

Such critiques of theatre determined neoclassical ideals of erudition and instruction – such as the respect for dramatic unity in literary traditions – and reinforced the mockery and containment of lower social classes. Renaissance plays thus describe stage actions in regulated terms such as 'fight scenes', 'clowning episodes', or 'processionals' and 'spectacles' rather than admit the suspect wanton movement of 'dancing', unattached to language or purpose. According to theatre historian Jonas Barish, what derives from the church and subsequent state censorship resides in 'a puritanical uneasiness about pleasure itself, and also a distrust of movement, which connects with ... an ideal of stasis in the moral and ontological realm' (Barish 1981: 135). Such 'anti-theatrical prejudice' has fatal effects upon theatre, as he further explains:

> [W]hatever exists in time, and unfolds in time, and utilizes human actors, must also involve motion as one of its mainsprings. To banish motion, to attempt to arrest or disguise it by ruling out the devices of stagecraft that exploit it, is in a sense to deny the intrinsically kinetic nature of the theatrical medium.
>
> (Barish 1981: 135)

Sadly, the effects of this hostility to movement in theatre were more damaging for women than men since their physical freedom in urban space was always curtailed. With the church's condemnation of public dancing, choreography also develops as a codified artistic form controlled by the court; hence neoclassical ideals of dance movement lead to opera and ballet but restrain the evolution of a more holistic idea of Western theatre. For those already 'corrupted' as actors or spectators, this period however ushers in a flourishing theatrical culture of playwrights, theatre venues and professional companies entertaining a broad-based popular audience.

Vernacular to cosmos: Renaissance theatre

Shakespeare produced no independent essays or commentaries on theatre. His theories of theatre have been debated and tested via the knowledge and experience of the plays and what is increasingly known about their historical context and staging conditions. New historicist scholars have provided metatheatrical commentary on performance traditions – Joseph Roach (1985) on the 'players' passion' or Stephen Greenblatt (1980) on 'renaissance self-fashioning' – thereby suggesting how Renaissance ideology or culture has informed the theatrical imagination, while materialist studies of production values, such as Siobhan Keenan's book *Acting Companies and Their Plays in Shakespeare's London* (2014), illuminate ideas about stage dramaturgy. Theories of movement across the extensive Renaissance repertoire also work at different levels, depending on the genre – whether comedy, history or tragedy – since each dramaturgy organizes stage action both visually and temporally within a defined space, establishing the status and relations between characters or radically shifting the horizon and perspectives on the stage world.

Assisting the representation of such diverse kinds of movement was the development of the 'plot' in Elizabethan theatre that provided a manuscript copy of the play, minus its dialogue, indicating when individual characters should enter scene by scene (Gurr 1996: 102). As with production scripts for blockbuster musicals, these schematic outlines helped producers to arrange stage props – to assist with the smooth flow of the action and prepare the actors for entries and exits. Hence 'plotting', in parallel with the development of mapping, became an intrinsic aspect of what we now call 'blocking', a system for managing, or codifying, stage movement in performance. If movement conventions were marked by the use of space, durational expectations were plotted across the arc of a scene or whole play; for instance, the sequence and number of exits and entrances, and whether in quick or slow succession, determine the precise rhythm of a dramatic situation. Think of the role of shouts or greetings in announcing a new arrival on stage, or in buying time for offstage business such as a costume change.

If the logics and circulation of print culture are indicative of movement conventions shaping stage reality, other features of Elizabethan society were also powerful determinants of its theatrical landscape. The changing social formation of cities and towns, which swelled with immigrants from the countryside and Europe, encouraged stage movement to represent scenes from everyday life, alongside the formalities of noble existence, and the realm of the other-worldly. The architecture and technologies of the playing space and the number and diverse range of actors were also conceptually shifting audience dynamics. Created for public theatres as well as the court, most plays needed to adapt to spaces of different sizes and shapes, and at the Globe, productions were seen by an audience that could be either pressed close to the edge of the stage or staggered above in the gallery looking down, thus entertained by the choreography of actors' legs and arms. The open playing space, the *platea*, became a key feature of dynamic actions, while the *skena*, or tiring-house at the rear – with its two opening side exit doors and third more central, curtained entry for processions, reveals or formal displays – provided a frame with which to construct movement tensions between one scene and another, as we saw in the Roman theatre. Dramatic group interactions were contrasted with cameo scenes, while performing outdoors provided opportunities for actors to develop an expressive acting style, as intense in close-up as it might be expansive in long view.

The spoken word often supports the spatio-temporal plotting, for instance, descriptions of actions taking place in an intimate sliver of space, such as a bower; an open field doing battle; or a country with unknown boundaries. In this way, articulated signals may point to the comportment of an individual actor or enhance the dynamics of an ensemble of soldiers or courtiers, fairies or clowns. The long history of these devices and the lack of reliance on fixed scenography have made Shakespeare's plays endlessly adaptable to modern theatre, as John Russell Brown suggests in his book *Shakespeare Dancing*, because each director can be 'mostly concerned with the relationship of actors to each other and their movements, both in groups and individually' (2005: 88). To examine in more detail how the dynamics of plot function, as well as how Shakespeare may have observed metropolitan movement vernacular, the following case study focuses on the volatile world of one of his later plays, *The Tempest*.

Case Study #4: *The Tempest* (1611, 2016)

Under the rule of King James I of England, the first production of *The Tempest* in 1611 coincides with the invention of new technologies of sight – the microscope (1590) and telescope (1608) – and new printing technologies that could circulate and report political and legal news as well as personal letters and diaries. The period was also inflected by the science of navigation with the mariner's compass essential for finding or losing one's bearings. The play draws upon these technologies of vision, news and geography to create an expanded horizon, to depict a world shaped somewhat randomly by storms and magical properties.

Let us consider Shakespeare's theory of movement through these diverse visual technologies, hence through the eyes of the shape-shifter Ariel from the play. Imagine he holds a kaleidoscope (invented two centuries later), made up of many tiny, coloured and beautiful crystals that align carefully within the frame but with a shake of the hand or a momentary shift of perspective, everything in the view-finder changes. Travelling from turbulence to calm, the narrative incorporates a multitude of movement tropes – the wildness of a storm, the pleasure of dancing, touches of intimacy, scenes of drunkenness, revenge action and magical flight – whose rapid shifting of energetic states is a driving force.

The opening scene dramatically establishes the turbulent motion of the storm, with the sailors strapped to the deck and arduously managing the sails while the noble travellers show their enfeebled anxiety. Short sentences punctuated by cries and swearing sounds from different parts of the stage, with the sailors aloft shouting instructions: 'To cabin! Silence! Trouble us not' (1.1.18–19) or 'Out of our way, I say!' (1.1.26) has a contrasting dynamic to the noblemen who run on and off for fear of drowning, crying 'We split, we split! – Farewell my wife and children!' (1.1.60–1).[1] The ship's rising and falling at sea is compared with the memory of 'an acre of barren ground – long heath, brown furze, anything' (1.1.66) now forsaken. In rapid succession, this volatile trajectory of splitting, pushing away, holding close and saying goodbye leads the audience from known ground to an uncertain, unmarked destiny.

Once the ship is wrecked, each scene turns like a fickle mariner's compass to 'another part of the isle', where different characters hide or take refuge. An apparently circular geography moves the play across landmarks, which enhances the sense that both characters and spectators are adrift or under a spell. Expanding the effects of Prospero's magic with different lenses, think here of the microscope and telescope in combination, collapses time and space while the spirit figure of Ariel transforms the movement of the heavens.

Having staged the freakish 'wild' nature of a storm and invited the suggestion of fleeting and ethereal movement,

The Tempest is also distinctive for what I call a metropolitan vernacular of stage movement. Along with an enlarging of the cosmic world, the density of the emerging metropolis of London places greater pressure on social relations, and much of the action relies upon relatively domestic, everyday dramas being exposed. The opening scene, for instance, portrays a distinctly tender and intimate conversation between father and daughter, Prospero and Miranda. Having learnt of her royal provenance, Miranda's discovery of the handsome prince Ferdinand enables the sensitive exploration of gestures animated by the sexuality of touch. To slow down the plot, Shakespeare interrupts their coupling when Prospero rebukes Ferdinand for courting Miranda's attentions. And there is little mistake about her intervening response that has a physical orientation:

MIRANDA   Beseech you, father –
PROSPERO
    Hence; hang not on my garments.

(1.2.473–74)

How easy it is to visualize the daughter clutching at her father and his reproach as embodied actions that push them apart, precipitating departure in different directions.

Such subtle familial relations are complemented by other character studies from London's teeming populace, 'of crowds and violent brawling, of drunkenness, of military discipline, religious practices and inhibitions, or personal courage and fear, and much else' (Brown 2005: 9). This vernacular movement was adapted to different physical types by individual actors, such as the clown Robert Armin or leading actor Richard Burbage from Shakespeare's company, often exploiting their discrete talents and traits for greater effect. Comedy in particular requires facial gestures and rustic tomfoolery whose meaning relies little on spoken language, and the quixotic, drunken and abusive behaviour of the sailors, Trinculo and Stephano, with the monster Caliban is movement humour at its most overt.

TRINCULO
By this light, a most perfidious and drunken
Monster; when god's asleep, he'll rob his bottle.
CALIBAN
I'll kiss thy foot. I'll swear myself thy subject.
STEPHANO
Come on, then, down and swear.
TRINCULO
I shall laugh myself to death at this puppy-
Headed monster. A most scurvy monster. I could find
In my heart to beat him.   (2.2.147–53)

Playing the dog, kissing a foot, rolling around with laughter provides plenty of scope for movement improvisation and invites the audience to recognize affinities between ordinary vulgar behaviour and theatrical experience. Having tackled drunkenness, the next scene, between the plotters Antony and Sebastian, examines another corporeal state that exists between two dimensions of consciousness. Under Ariel's spell, they cannot help falling asleep, so the two men talk themselves towards the edge of oblivion, slowly giving in to the heavy disintegration of the body and drifting thoughts:

SEBASTIAN
This is a strange repose, to be asleep
With eyes wide open – standing, speaking, moving,
And yet so fast asleep.
....
Well, I am standing water.
ANTONIO
I'll teach you how to flow.
SEBASTIAN   Do so. To ebb
Hereditary sloth instructs me. (2.1.213–23)

With room for variation in the embodiment and delivery, the sense of physical exhaustion generates the atmosphere of sleep. Out of this stupor, Antonio suddenly realizes that 'ebbing men' might become too fearful, lazy or dispirited, in 'standing water', and what greater ambition he would have if he were to become king. Snapping out of his torpor with a shout of energy, he calls his mate to draw his sword. From the drooping shoulders and sagging legs of his 'strange repose', the surging power of such alert waking affirms Shakespeare's acute, and closely lived, observation of vernacular movement.

According to Brown, this 'realism' in Shakespeare's later plays had to be 'performative and embodied in the physical presence of the actors' (2005: 156). Representation begins to require corporeal eloquence and becomes essential for scenes in which a glance or someone stepping aside suggests something too ghastly to depict. At other times, the use of 'silence' might involve considerable movement on stage, such as during a banquet with the 'routine activities' of people serving food, licking fingers, clinking glasses, clearing plates or whispering (2005: 158). Such mimed actions, or 'dumb shows', remain more common in ballet and opera whereas naturalistic theatre has often allocated the scoring of movement-only scenes to the minor roles. Vernacular rhythms can however inform the mood of a play because they provide sensory interactions with objects which reveal diverse social relations underpinning the theatre experience.

Theatre phenomenologist Bert O. States considers that Shakespeare excelled in this choreography of successive movement, in what might be regarded as a process of 'composing for the actor' (1985: 131). *The Tempest*'s panoply of vernacular movement – ordinary people doing familiar things – must have moved its public. Keenan writing about Shakespeare's audiences notes that their pleasure was often marked by loud laughter, while 'distaste included hissing, calling out and even throwing missiles' (2014: 147). This animated transmission, itself a form of movement, might be likened to an 'autopoetic loop', in the terms of theatre scholar Erika Fischer-Lichte, since 'the audience's physical participation is set in motion through synaesthetic perception, shaped not only by sight and sound but by physical sensations of the entire body' (2008: 36).

Given the extraordinary turbulence of *The Tempest*, what is exciting, then, is that the movement score imagines both the synaesthetic perception of ordinary behaviours as well as the relentless sense of energetic planetary motion. The smaller, more intimate scenes that I described earlier must contend with the concentration of time passing and the feeling of instability suggested by the larger themes of the play. Both made and unmade by magic, the individual characters become defined by these cameo physical portraits, while it is those measures of space and techniques of perception – the compass spinning and the telescope and microscope sharpening our sight – that assemble the wider durational effects of the whole as a movement of physical, moral and social transformation.

Since *The Tempest*'s Prospero is King of Milan, the character of Grand Duke Ferdinand could represent the son of the Renaissance ruler, Cosimo de Medici. A great lover of theatre and music, Cosimo generously staged a three-week cycle of fetes for his own son's wedding, and its ethereal, other-worldly 'intermezzi' reinstated the 'ancient' effects of thematic unity with conceptions of divine justice (Strong 1973: 179). The instigators of such remarkable spectacles were philosophers, engineers, scientists and artists, including, at the court of King James in England, the playwright Ben Jonson and designer Inigo Jones. A compatriot and rival of Shakespeare, Jonson observed of one of these magnificent spectacles:

No less to be admired, for the grace and greatness was the whole machine of the spectacle, from whence they came, the first part of which was a mikrokosmos, or globe, filled with countries, and those gilded; where the sea was exprest, heightened with silver waves ...

But that which (as above in place, so in the beauty) was most taking in the spectacle was the sphere of fire, in the top of all, encompassing the air, and imitated with such art and industry as the spectators might discern the motion (all the time the shows lasted) without any mover.

(Jonson 1838: 559)

Shakespeare may have used the image of theatre as a 'globe', but for Jonson's globe, the movement of the moon and planets, illuminated by means of air, fire, water and metals, was centred around the glory of the king. Designer Jones's expert knowledge of turning implements, such as wheels and gears, reflected the heightened interest in instruments of motion within the Renaissance, but for the poet Jonson, the motor of propulsion, its *machina versatilis*, should be hidden from the audience, hence allowing the sovereign to be 'imagined as the driving mechanical force', for the mystery of the spheres (Sawday 2007: 158).

The influence of these new conceptions of royal power within Europe and this Renaissance machinery for flights of imagination have unmistakeable influence on *The Tempest*, most manifest in Ariel's willingness to move in whatever way Prospero commands:

> I come
> To answer thy best pleasure, be't to fly,
> To swim, to dive into the fire, to ride
> On the curled clouds. To thy strong bidding, task
> Ariel and all his quality. (1.2.189–93)

With this history of spectacle, the recent collaboration between the Royal Shakespeare Company (RSC), the global internet company Intel and Imaginarium Studio, for an intermedial production of *The Tempest* in 2016, is not so surprising. With high production values, and extensive use of virtual reality (VR) technology, the performance experimented with motion capture and animation to transform the stage with digital projections of the ship's hull and unseen island landscapes. The play's fantasy visions of magic or non-human presences also inspired Ariel, appropriately, to appear as a translucent avatar.

Following the domestic scene between Miranda and Prospero described earlier, Prospero commands Ariel:

Go make thyself like a nymph o'th' sea;
Be subject to no sight but thine and mine, invisible
To every eyeball else. Go take this shape
And hither come in't. Go! Hence with diligence. (1.2.302–05)

To become this 'nymph ... subject to no sight but thing and mine' the actor Mark Quartley playing Ariel was hooked up via a motion-capture suit so that he simultaneously appears on his feet, and his 'shape invisible' (4.1.185) flies around the stage. Motion capture, as Nicholas Salazar-Sutil notes, 'synthesizes the qualities of puppetry, live action, stop-motion animation, game intelligence, and other forms into an entirely new fusion that can play freely with quantifiable movement – not just the image of movement' (2015: 204). Quartley's facial expressions are also filmed and replayed through digital loops, partially controlled by the actor in real time. Distributing these effects across the mise en scène with changes of light, speed, colour and programmed segmentation of the recorded data, Ariel appears to 'swim', 'dive' and 'ride' in the air above and beyond Prospero's head, so he is truly able to goad the magician from all corners of the stage world.

This continuous movement of bodily data, translated into pixelated images, adds to the audience's fantasy of Ariel, both as a figment of imagination and as the disembodied and provoking voice of Prospero's conscience. The theatrical 'entanglement of movement and technology' has many wonders but Prospero knows when enough is enough (Salazar-Sutil and Popat 2015: 4):

Our revels now are ended. These our actors,
As I foretold you, were all spirits and
Are melted into air, into thin air; (4.1.148–50)

The Shakespearean imagination of worlds turning within worlds was realized in this *RSC Tempest* with all the artifice of light, projections, circular motion, and spatial and corporeal mapping that Renaissance artists, such as Jones and Jonson, might have both admired and scorned. Indeed, the contemporary audience watched with awe as the concept of virtual movement seemed echoed by the text: 'the Nymphs in a graceful dance ... ; after which, to a strange hollow and confused noise, they heavily vanish' (4.1.138 SD). And with a push of the VR operator's button, they did indeed vanish. Hence, the expansive Renaissance imagination has given theatre multiple ways to think about movement – observation of the domestic and vernacular movements of the city, as well as the interaction between machines and the corporeal as the motor for spectacle. The complexity of these theories of movement – on the one hand, realizing the subtlety in daily life, and on the other, reaching out to the heavens or cosmos – continues to cascade into contemporary theatre.

Automata and puppets: theatres of science

By the eighteenth century, with the rise of a sophisticated urban society, European culture changes dynamic. Intellectually, new instruments of capital, science and creativity invent taxonomies, new world discoveries and bureaucracies of state, as well as transformational technologies such as steam engines, printing presses and electricity. The Enlightenment individual becomes of heightened political, social and artistic significance, and concepts of citizenship and subjectivity sit alongside Romantic ideals of artistic expressive autonomy. In terms of theatre, theories that previously upheld the tumultuousness of a courtly world, in thrall to divine or symbolic intervention, were replaced by world views that reason, and science, could explain the effects of movement, whether identifying the nervous system or seeing planets revolve. Scientific advances saw inventors and scientists presenting public lectures with assistants demonstrating their experiments with a 'raising of levers, hauling at pulleys and turning of globes' (Coppola 2016: 128). The fascinations of chemistry, astronomy, physics and biology were however a challenge to accepted understandings of the centrality of the human in philosophy and hence also in theatre.

Theatre historian Al Coppola argues that with science offering such exciting presentations to the public, the London stage responded with popular theatrical entertainments that were pseudo-scientific, such as necromancy, feats of extreme strength, hypnosis and séances. A popular theme for eighteenth-century plays was variations on Christopher Marlowe's *Dr Faustus*, an Elizabethan tragedy that depicts a learned scholar who does a deal with the devil over his own soul, and Faustus becomes recast as a tragicomic Harlequin in both *The Necromancer* and *The Beggars' Opera*. Other unscripted performances saw leading actors perform as 'conjurors' by bringing in dragons, the Hell-mouth and pyrotechnics – 'a fire, a jig, a battel and a ball' – to thrill audiences (2016: 131). Documenting these anarchic productions, Coppola argues that in this rapidly modernizing culture, the medium of theatre may have quite literally mesmerized its spectators so that 'the modern, technological magic of the Harlequin Faustus' becomes associated 'with the more contemporary modern magic of natural philosophy – particularly the public science of popular Newtonianism' (2016: 128).

Scientific objectivity in its more sober form governs the conduct of human physiology and social behaviour. The Roman physician Galen developed the theory of the body shaped by humours that flowed around the body affecting our moods, an idea that influenced medicine and religious thought for nearly 1,500 years. The Galenic vitalism of blood ebbing and flowing with cosmic cycles 'known to God alone' was however replaced by an anatomical heart when William Harvey registered 'the quickness of the motion' in its pumping valves (1628: 1–2). Mechanical in shape and action, the heart must be relinquished as a symbol of inner constancy, becoming then a component within a dynamic system of internal corporeal movement. Two centuries later when natural scientist Charles Darwin develops the theory of evolution, the observation of movement in humans, animals and plants underpins the thesis. One small detail of seedling roots pushing through the soil describes them as 'more strongly pronounced in radicals when they first protrude from the seed than at a later period' (Darwin 1880: 71–2). The subtle notes of movement observation, as they were for Aristotle, become significant to scientific enquiry, helping Darwin to explain the shift of humans from crawling animals to bipedalism as evolution.

Scientific legitimacy also binds theories of motion to natural forces which may be harnessed to ideological conceptions. In moral philosophy, Adam Smith writing in 1759, for instance, compares the requirements of a harmonious society with a movement machine:

> We naturally confound it in our imagination with the order, the regular and harmonious movement of the system, the machine or economy by means of which it is produced ... It is well that nature imposes upon us in this manner. It is this deception which rouses and keeps in continual motion the industry of mankind.
>
> (Smith 2004: 108)

The wheels of society either turn smoothly or grumble along causing toil, anxiety and offence. Such moral analysis of movement extends next to character, and the Swiss physiognomist Johann Kaspar Lavater's theories were widely quoted: 'each individual has his character, and every character has a physiognomy proper to it'; it is this physical appearance which gives 'tone to the look, to the gesture, to the carriage, to the mien, to the gait, to all our movements active and passive' (Markley and Wallace 2016: 105). Individuals are thus divided from one another by the correspondence between external and internal countenance. The visible signs of vice or virtue, attitude or emotional propensity, can be 'read'; flickering eye movements could signify 'short or weak sight, fear and care', while bright eyes, slow of motion, 'bespeak the hero, great acts, audacious, cheerful, one feared by his enemies' (Lavater 1866: 55).

This idea that we know the person through their outward conduct and even by their involuntary movements still has a pernicious hold on our assessment of character. What 'a man becomes at particular moments', writes Lavater, can exude tranquil strength in stillness while active strength involves motion which is 'elastic'; mostly a sign of virility, too much active strength may produce 'the living power of irritability', particularly from those with a 'certain kind of stiffness' (1866: 28–9). On the other hand, the rapid motion of some characters can be deceptive and have the opposite effect of 'charming' or 'superior' (Lavater 1866: 243). In terms of theatre, the influence of physiognomy was to create a system of stereotypes that attributed physical signs to character 'manifested by the moveable parts in motion' of gait, gesture, alignment and agitation (Lavater 1866: 26). If physiognomy taught knowledge of character in the bodily signs, pathognomy went even further as it tried to determine the location of genius, 'whether understanding be in the eye-bone, wit in the chin, and poetical genius in the mouth' (Markley and Wallace 2016: 168). Such moral judgement for those who imitate the bodily conduct of others or exhibit defaulting behaviours circulates across theatre and performance into the nineteenth century. Famous actors such as Garrick would try to produce portraits concerned with the 'minutiae of theatrical presentation' which, as art historian Shearer West suggests, was no escape from the approbation of physiognomy as a discourse on character or the 'movements of the soul' (1991: 3). Perhaps, then, it is not surprising that the study of the actor and movement became itself a topic of scientific curiosity, attention and psychological analysis in theatre theory.

When the French essayist and playwright Denis Diderot produced his multi-volume *Encyclopaedia* (1751–66), it included many theatre entries. In his famous essay on the 'paradox of the actor', he suggests that a 'sublime actor' lacks 'sensibility', which means that an actor should communicate through their body without feeling the emotions they depict. But he also suggests there may be a sensibility at a cellular level which affectively corresponds to the emotion portrayed: 'I can perceive that with a certain arrangement and a certain movement in the smallest particles of this body, there exists a correlation between the body and the impression it makes upon me' (Diderot and d'Alembert 2003: 24–7). What Diderot sketches here is the more contemporary theory that inner kinaesthetic perception coordinates with physical responses that can produce affective and cognitive responses for the actor and audience. Cautious however about this hypothesis, he suggests that the senses are unreliable in shaping any constant understanding of movement: 'Reason and experience teach us that bodies are in a continuous state of movement or change which is frequently quite imperceptible', he marvels, and 'the body can alter and so can I' (Diderot and d'Alembert 2003: 24–7). As with Aristotle, so for Diderot, a body's capacity for change, for making and giving impressions of distance, shape and duration, operates within a wider set of ideas about movement and human experience. This conception of the senses as only one aspect of movement apprehension, and the notion of imperceptible qualities affecting corporeal transformation, expands the paradox of the actor to that of a sensitive register for the complexity of embodied performance – a notion that we will consider more fully in Section Two when we examine systems of actor training.

In as much as the eighteenth century embraced public fascination with new social and scientific ideas, a wider scepticism about the central importance of the organic human to society began to appear. Diderot's associate, Jean-Baptiste d'Alembert, identifies, for instance, the movement potential of a flying duck and a wind-up flute player on exhibition in the Paris Academy of Sciences as that of the 'Automaton: Instrument which moves by itself, or machine which contains within itself the source of its motion. The word comes from the Greek αὐτόματον and is composed of αὐτὸς ipse [sic], and μάω, "I am excited, ready to move," or perhaps μάτην, "easily," from which came αὐτόματος "spontaneous," "voluntary"' (Diderot and d'Alembert 2003: 896–7). How is it that invisible currents can send sparks flying or make bodies seem to levitate? Once mechanical systems appear to have autonomous movement, then what they represent or substitute for human movement becomes of interest to the theatre.

In his essay 'On the Marionette Theatre' in 1810, German writer Heinrich von Kleist recounts how puppets might be better dancers than humans:

> Each movement ... will have a centre of gravity; it would suffice to say to direct this crucial point to the inside of the figure. The limbs that function as nothing more than a pendulum, swinging freely, will follow the movement in their own fashion without anyone's aid.
>
> (Kleist 1972: 22)

Although limited by the vertical force of gravity, 'those movements of which they are capable are accomplished with a composure, lightness, and grace that would amaze any sensitive observer' (1972: 23). For Kleist, while the controlling puppeteer must understand the purely mechanical, the approximations of movements through lines, ellipses and parabolas, and hence 'would never be guilty of affection', paradoxically the grace of puppet movement cannot be 'managed entirely without some feeling' (1972: 23).

If Kleist proposed that puppet movement might liberate human subjectivity from self-conscious failure to attain 'grace', the French avant-garde author and playwright Alfred Jarry, writing a century later, saw the puppet as the answer to the 'futility' of a theatre that had become stuffed with an excess of fake gestures and over-blown sentiment. His essays and trio of plays featuring the 'ignoble creature' Monsieur Ubu provide commentary on the instability of wars in Europe, in a history that becomes 'ridiculously' dependent on theatre as mere salve for decadent conduct. Rather than mimic reality, Jarry calls for an abstract theatre that could examine 'pataphysical' reality, that is, a universe shaped by the pseudo-science of corrupting forces, against which we must 'strike out with all our arms of pschittical, phynancial and physical varieties' (Jarry 1965: 37). His scatological invention of a new theatre is contingent upon rejection of social propriety and theatrical convention; hence the actor must learn to utilize stage technologies, such as masks and lighting, to greater effect: 'By slow nodding and lateral movements of his head the actor can displace the shadows over the whole surface of his mask. And experience has shown that the six main positions ... suffice for every expression' (1965: xxv). Arguing against the sentimental gestures of mime, Jarry expects the marionette to restrict themselves to a repertoire of 'universal expressions' such as 'displaying its bewilderment by starting back violently and hitting its head against a flat' (1965: xxv). Knocking oneself out by moving backwards cannot be performed by a live actor but it can produce both funny and terrifying connotations when enacted by a puppet.

Jarry's preface for *Ubu Roi* (1896) expands upon these core principles. The setting in Poland was indicated by a placard rather than conventional painted scenography; a crowd was not a mass of people pretending to behave in unison but could be represented by one soldier shooting a gun. Whizzing cannon balls and bodies being torn to pieces can never be fully enacted on stage, but 'a handful of pulleys and strings serve to control a whole army of marionettes' (1965: xxviii). Jarry laments that he could not replace all his actors with marionettes but made 'cardboard masks for the actors of Ubu, who were talented enough to depersonalize themselves voluntarily' (1965: xxvii). His childlike cartoons of a figure with a bag over his head and holes cut for haunted eyes have become the prototype for the actor replaced by a deadly mask since they resemble the hooded capes of the Klu Klux Klan. For Jarry, however, the excesses of dictatorship, or anonymous power, can be manifest anywhere, hence the type is best revealed by 'the impassivity of the mask', since it is in the shadows and effects that can be generated through animation of the mask that 'its tragicomic qualities have always been acknowledged' (1965: xxv). The puppet figure thus animates a complex politics rather than being an object invested with animated subjectivity. In contemporary forms of puppet theatre, the puppet on strings and the puppet with a supernatural life are both explored as the following case study of *War Horse* suggests.

Case Study #5: *War Horse* (2007)

The Handspring Theatre Company from South Africa has developed the sophisticated use of the puppet-automaton in many of their productions. Their version of the Ubu play, called *Ubu and the Truth Commission* (1997) featured puppets that were dogs and crocodiles snapping at the heels of a grotesquely bigoted white Ubu, in which the shadow of Kleist and Jarry's challenge to the theatre took on the trappings of the apartheid system of power. If Jarry was a precursor for the grotesque malevolence of mechanical toys in Handspring's *Ubu*, then, as Kleist suggests, the movements of such animals also 'perform a dance that neither he nor any other outstanding dancer … could equal' (1972: 23). Many more spectators have had a similar experience of watching the 'dance' of Handspring puppets in the National Theatre's acclaimed production *War Horse* (2007), which has toured the world since its inception. Based on a children's book by Michael Morpurgo adapted for the stage by Nick Stafford (2007), the play tells the story of the horses that carried British soldiers to and from the front during the First World War, and alongside human actors, this globally acclaimed production was animated by large-scale, life-like puppet animals.

Constructed of bent canes, tied and jointed with wires, the ribbed horse skeletons have realistic vertebrae, and extended cables lift the head, move the ears and turn the eyes. Mesh around the outer frame gives the body of the horse a surface skin and the tail is made of leather strips. The tensile supports are turned and pulled to lift the horses' heads or establish a trotting action by the three actor–puppeteers – one each for the head, heart and hind legs – as they learn to breathe together and synchronize the physical responses of the horse to the stage action. Rehearsals that attend to minor movements appear enlarged on stage and involve defining the characteristics of the animal bodies as much as learning any script or how to 'act'. According to Kleist, a subtle relationship exists between the movements of the puppeteer's fingers and 'those of the attached puppets, somewhat like the relationship of numbers to logarithms or the asymptote to the hyperbola' (1972: 23). The puppets' connection to gravity is a straight line, as he further explains, but with the skills of 'symmetry, mobility, lightness' executed by the puppeteers, the horses develop an eerie quality – disciplined, resilient and neurotic – somehow more universal and less time-bound (1972: 24).

The transformative effects of mechanical movements in *War Horse* command the forces of gravity that enable a structure to move, a complex process of studying the physical displacements of limbs and realizing the transfer of weight that will make the puppet horses walk, run and collapse convincingly. Nothing of Jarry's grotesque, but rather we see the uncanniness of a leather and wooden horse at larger than human size with its eight legs (two humans, four suspended) being ridden by a person. Minus the animator and resting on the floor, however, the lifeless mask is haunting, the ghost body of a dead horse, with its glassy eyes staring at the ceiling.

For many children (and adults), watching Joey, the much-loved horse of the young soldier Albert, was a mesmerizing experience that, like Kleist's narrator, invited the audience to suspend judgement about the reality of the horse and its relationship to the senseless violence of war. In one scene, the young man Albert talks to his horse Joey, craning his neck to look into the majestic animal's eyes. He also grips the neck brace as if he himself is holding its reins rather than lifting the horse's head four feet into the air. At other times, the head operators literally dance around the horses which trot together, as if communing with one another – and the stresses felt by the horses metamorphose into the field of movement on stage. One of the strengths of the production are these human-puppet interactions, just as is the case with a ventriloquist who makes us believe that the puppet sitting on their lap is not animated by them but has its own voice and independent gestures.

As the story progresses into the grim reality of conflict, the mobile energies of the horse's fallen head, the sure-footed elegance of a proud gallop and its slow heaving walk convey the very real dramas of the war. A scenario like arriving in a field or lining up for a march through a village has its specific, cumbersome temporal dimension that becomes peculiarly absorbing. Think, for instance, of watching a dog greet its owner, or a line of ants climbing along a plant tendril – whether quick or slow, such ambulations have their own pace and fascination. The experience of young boys far from home, with their sense of confusion in the trenches as bombs fall around them, is also communicated by the tenderness with which the puppeteers care for these horses made of wood, wire and cloth. When Joey is trapped by barbed wire and close to death towards the end of the war, often the audience is crying, having transferred their affective responses from the human to the horse.

The *War Horse* audience must believe in this expert imitation of movement in the puppet, while they also admire the virtuosic muscularity of the operators, like gymnasts on a training horse, restrained by the puppet. To the extent that the automatons give pleasure and grace to movement sensations, their performance is neither an echo nor a direct response to the reality of flesh and blood actors, as such they can depersonalize yet exaggerate the sentiments of human cruelty, greed or hurt. The puppets therefore ventriloquize the innocent (Albert) and the soldiers' muted voices, speaking about things that are difficult to express, and so they represent the human experience of war in which ordinary people are like puppets too. To be critical of the machinery of war, the role of the puppets is therefore doubled, asking for identification with the animals, while asserting the tacit nature of our manipulation. Such dual awareness of mechanical or puppet movement in the theatre has become increasingly critical as the power of animation extends into dialogue with the live actor, as we discussed in *The Tempest*, in the genres of virtual reality and animation.

Conclusion

To conclude this chapter, let us recap how an understanding of movement within the theatre interacts with and represents changes in historical time. We began with the enriched sense of the chorus as a movement genre or formation, expressive of and attuned to the complexity of rhythms – their beats and discords – in ancient Greek society and have ended with a transfer of mobility and action to the puppet faced with the machinery of war. We have also travelled far and wide in the observation of movement, from the performance of religious or street events to the diverse world of cities and courts in East and West and I have emphasized ensemble movements, whether performed as rituals, processions or cosmic spectacles. Detailed articulation of actor movement has also been the focus during selected periods – non-Western philosophies of theatre offering complex understanding of the uses of movement in performance, while moral judgements upon the unruliness, and character, of corporeal movement have shaped theatre history. How actors move, and how they acquire the nuances of theatrical gesture and character representation, I would suggest, provides significant insight into the prescriptions of different cultural and historical ideologies.

In this rapid overview of three millennia of theatre, we see that movement is always subject to judgements of value that construct and shape the actions appearing on stage, and these judgements will be historically determined and never static.

Any interpretation of theatrical movement will depend on the imaginative negotiation of figurative relations between stage and actor, bodies and energies, pace and plot, mind and machine, audience and social context. Whether movements are copied from life – closely observed as inner sensations and reproduced outwardly via imitation – or replicated (and perhaps replaced) by artificial extensions, theories of movement provide valuable ways to consider how theatre contributes to historical understanding.

SECTION TWO

Movement Systems and Embodied Action

Characterized by the pulse and energy of ever-new forms of scientific and social machinery – cars and aeroplanes, sports and space travel – movement in the twentieth century represented a new and exhilarating mode for seeing and experiencing reality. Arts such as cinema, dance and television were experimenting with aesthetic representations of motion, kinaesthesia and motility, hence exploring ideas that have become central to philosophy, sociology and cultural studies. And theatre and performance were artistic leaders of modernist innovations that would shape radically different assumptions about how movement, gesture and other forms of mobility communicate with audiences.

Given these turbulent artistic and social transformations, this section will examine how concepts of movement in theatre developed distinctive movement systems and embodied practices. In some systems, human movement represents the special authenticity of the individual; for others movement knowledge is an exhilarating component of a technological economy, but across theatrical genres from naturalism to participatory theatre, the sources and meanings attributed to movement represent an important field of enquiry. The term *system* is here understood to denote that combination of ideas, methods, beliefs and values that inhere in a cultural group but, as with scientific methodologies, such concepts are developed through practices that include testing, training, making, assembling or presenting their inherent 'truths', 'bias' or 'hypotheses'. Each system attempts to embody a particular view of the human being and its purpose within theatre or in society, and the systems discussed include the holistic, the mechanical, the dynamic and the esoteric. We will examine these approaches in relation to a range of key figures of twentieth-century theatre – Konstantin Stanislavski, Vsevolod Meyerhold, Bertolt Brecht, Jerzy Grotowski – and extend our examination with case studies of historically significant productions of *Hedda Gabler*, *Mother Courage* and *The Constant Prince* as well as discussion of more contemporary productions such as *Operation Orfeo*, *About Kazuo Ohno* and *Audience*.

Holistic systems: Craig, Delsarte and Dalcroze

The first decades of the twentieth century were exciting times, with calls for a 'new theatre' resounding across Europe. The English theatre designer Edward Gordon Craig, for instance, rejected the rhetorical acting styles of melodramatic theatre and believed that movement would help to reinvent theatre and performance. In this belief, he was inspired by modern dancers such as Isadora Duncan who offered her body as the fullest expression of 'the poetry of movement' when she danced in Grecian tunics with free-flowing gestures in the open air. According to Craig, theatre should be able to mould poetic images of storms and sunsets, troops of soldiers and heavenly nymphs, as well as give form to the innermost 'thoughts and emotions of the particular character' (1977: 22). Indeed, Craig railed against conventional or popular theatre and exalted the inner qualities of movement that might convey higher truths:

In the beginning with you it was Impersonation: you passed on to Representation, and now you advance into Revelation. When Impersonating and Representing you made use of those materials which have always been made use of; that is to say, the human figure as exemplified in the actor, speech as exemplified in the poet through the actor, the visible world as shown by means of Scene. You now will reveal by means of movement the Invisible things ... those seen through the eye and not with the eye, by the wonderful and divine power of Movement.

(Craig 1977: 32–3)

Symbolist expression through movement and stagecraft was designed to transcend mundane existence. Rather than restrict theatre to ideas about the emotional attributes of character or mannerist spectacle, Craig believed in the consciousness that movement could evoke through 'the mask', as his description of actor Henry Irving suggests:

Try and conceive for yourself that face in movement ... movement which was ever under the powerful control of the mind. Can you not see the mouth being made to move by the brain, and that same movement which is called expression creating a thought as definite as the line of a draughtsman does on a piece of paper or as a chord does in music? Cannot you see the slow turning of those eyes and the enlargement of them? These two movements alone contained so great a lesson for the future of the art of the theatre.

(1977: 15)

With his close description of Irving's eyes rolling and enlarging, Craig intimates an understanding of relations between body and thought, form and intention that were, as we shall see in this section, to become central to concepts of the actor and stagecraft. This observation also signals an important shift towards a more holistic relationship to movement as the inner vitality of artistic expression, an approach closely identified with scientific naturalism, and of a modern drama seeking to reveal the truths of character. From henceforth, the formal systems of theatre engage more systematically with movement in the rehearsal studio and in the preparation of actors for performance.

Across Europe, theatre training schools became associated with theatre companies, and a wide range of physical education systems were developed for actors and dancers to apply learnt poses and techniques to theatrical expression. Defining the integrity of such systems, their teachers often sought legitimation through classical and Romantic ideals of dramatic expression and above all through claims to a holistic view of the person. The French music teacher François Delsarte (1811–71) devised an elaborate philosophical system at the end of the nineteenth century in which the body was regarded as a spiritual instrument while the Swiss music educator Emile Jacques-Dalcroze (1865–1950) placed emphasis on rhythmic patterns that became the movement and music system today called Eurhythmics. Both artists have continuing influence on movement education in theatre today, because what lies at the core of these methods is a belief that the body, mind and soul are one and that the individual can be transformed in a unifying way through attention to at first physical training and then other aspects of their mental and spiritual life.

Delsarte, for instance, conceived of a complex tripartite philosophy in which macrocosm and microcosm were defined by the 'Law of Correspondence' that shaped relations between the body and spiritual world. Zones of the body were aligned with 'Great Orders of Movement' represented by 'Oppositions, Parallelisms [and] Successions' (which includes specific actions such as 'Bowing and Falling') (Shawn 1974: 27). Governed by 'Nine Laws of Motion', his system provided a way to organize movement states according to scientific principles that could be observed and modified. Most valuably for theatre, the translation of Delsarte's theory into performance recognized that the human subject was never static in attitude or expression but could shift smoothly in response to internal or external stimuli.

Genevieve Stebbins, a North American teacher of the Delsarte System of Expression, developed sequenced exercises designed to activate consciousness of small movements and corporeal orientations. Her method begins with a series of exercises for 'decomposing' the bad physical habits of a stance: positioning the feet apart, she instructs the student on slight adjustments to the inclination of head or torso, carefully followed by the spine, the gaze, and a shifting of weight through the soles of the feet (Stebbins 1977: 83). This sequence is probably familiar to most student theatre practitioners today as a basic warm-up technique, and a similar assembling of kinaesthetic awareness of subtle movement continues through an exploration of various body parts, from the central axis to the extremities. Stebbins accompanies this physical study with a growing appreciation of the 'attitudes' that might be composed and combined to express powerful states of mind. Hence, Delsartism offered a means to learn the 'grammar of pantomime', without becoming too prescriptive about any intended dramatic performance. With echoes of Quintilian's rhetorical gestures speaking more than words, Delsarte and his followers elevated the poetics of gesture beyond a mere physical training to a spiritual project that could be aligned with Platonic concepts of movement 'harmonized' to a higher ideal of divine grace and 'delighting power' (Shawn 1974: 25). By proposing that corporeal improvement could contribute to the elevation of human knowledge, the theory embodied by this holistic movement philosophy helped remove the social stigma that was often attached to ideas that acting was corrupting and duplicitous.

Another reformer, Dalcroze, recognized that rhythmic movement could be a prerequisite for theatre experimentation and pioneered the coordination of bodily rhythms with the learning of complex musical patterns. Precise acoustic exercises, such as clapping and following a drum-beat, stopping or starting with the variations in a musical phrase, or differentiating the embodied quality of a musical forte and pianissimo, create endless variations for expressive movement, with some of his students complaining of 'fatiguing complexity' (Toepfer 1997: 119). In their formal alignment with musical structure, this system of training resisted the symbolic idealism of the Delsarte poses and opened up movement exploration to interdisciplinary studies with architecture, lighting, theatre history and, of course, musicality.

During the 1920s, Dalcroze and his collaborators opened an arts school in the German industrial city of Hellerau in which experimental theatre productions and large outdoor spectacles could radically trial new technologies and methods. The theatre designer Adolphe Appia built a unique stage arrangement of large blocks – recombined as towers or plateaus – that was both stage and auditorium. Set on the tiers, a movement chorus had to manifest dramatic ideas in a vertical abstract choreography deployed as 'decoration'. In 1913, following demonstrations of rhythmic gymnastics and 'plastic music representations', Christoph Willibald Gluck's 1762 opera, *Orpheus and Eurydice*, was staged for a 5,000-strong audience that included European theatre luminaries and intellectuals such as George Bernard Shaw, Max Reinhardt, Rudolf Laban, Mary Wigman, Constantin Stanislavski, Serge Diaghilev and Marie Rambert. Reviewers praised the 'plastic sense' of the performance, the light and the music, which 'possesses them both physically and emotionally'; however, 'most impressive of all was the naturalness' of the choreography (Roesner 2016: 52). In its elegant simplicity of stage and lighting design, the choral movement seems to have produced an impressionistic panorama, adding to the perceptual dimensions of a theatre aesthetics built around movement composition as much as narrative structure.

Case Study #1: *Operation Orfeo* (1993)

The contemporary production of *Operation Orfeo* (1993, 2007, 2021) by the Danish theatre collective Hotel Pro

Forma resembles this utopian choral movement experiment. With a libretto that narrates the legend of Orpheus trying to rescue the nymph Eurydice from the underworld and a score which includes Gluck's orchestration as well as English and French *a capella* singing, the stage is designed as a series of steps or terraces. The production begins with nothing more than the darkened stage surrounded by a white frame, a stark arrangement that shuts down visual perception and concentrates the audience's attention on the swelling music. After about twenty minutes sufficient red lighting seeps onto the stage to reveal an ensemble of shadowy figures standing and sitting on horizontal striations within the picture box. Wearing black cloaks and pointed hats, they could be undertakers or members of a strange sect, and they slowly rearrange themselves on different levels – sometimes one with five standing below or perhaps three lying down with another three seated on each step above. Subtle lighting changes, such as a tone of white becoming slighter cooler, variously throws the group formations into shadow or covers them with bands of colour. With the spectators' senses heightened by these minimalist adjustments, the smallest or slowest of movements, such as one figure walking across a plane, or all of them opening their arms together, disturbs the whole arrangement.

Each moving sculptural form in this 'conceptual opera' – illuminated by these tonal variations of colour, shape and music – generates a dramatic intensity that transfers affectively to the audience. At one moment, the red washes suggest something terrible; at others the clustering of figures seems to be embedded in a womb. I imagine *Operation Orfeo* resembling the aesthetics of the Hellerau production, since the shifting between each state, or scene, with its subtle movement transitions produces a series of haunting, somewhat ethereal effects – longing, foreboding and mourning – that unfold the fateful love story within the most abstract of representations. A woman descending the stairs, for example, while the chorus stands to watch her pass by, drains the spectator of hope. With almost no action, and only the choral mutability of the stage on offer, Craig, Appia and

Dalcroze might have also been impressed by this contemporary realization of their lyrical and holistic vision for movement in the theatre.

Vitality: Bergson and Merleau-Ponty

While theatre artists were experimenting with new forms of movement expression and composition in the early twentieth century, and as social life became more rapidly industrial, new intellectual projects were aimed at understanding the phenomenal world of movement. Writing in 1907, the philosopher Henri Bergson evoked the inner streams that give rise to the vitality of experience. For Bergson, human beings – and indeed all things that grow, evolve and change – have intrinsic vitality and we therefore experience matter not through its inertness but through the pulse and energetic shifts that living things make as they turn towards and away from light or gravity. Human subjectivity is constituted, as Bergson explains in his book *Matter and Memory* (1991), through consciousness of movement. The brain and cerebral activity that shape awareness of self will evolve into 'memory-images' formed through 'movements' which 'prolong our perception in order to bring from it useful effects, and thus *take us away* from the object perceived' while at the same time and in a contra-motion, 'they *bring* us back to the object, to dwell upon its outlines' (1991: 98). The phenomenology of movement between objects and images thus becomes central to consciousness itself, as well as to the embodied experience of vitality and creativity.

Ideas of the perceptual, the moving and the energetic aspects of creativity suggest a distinction between, on the one hand, the role that semiotics and psychoanalysis have played in the interpretation of twentieth-century theatre and, on the other, the contribution of phenomenology. What is at stake for theatre, and our understanding of movement, in relation to the science of phenomena in which the human being is one among many other things that have life? What do we mean when we associate human consciousness, the distinct sense of being a self, with a unique body? How do we encounter the world we inhabit? These questions about the role of consciousness and embodied movement in the constitution of both experience and knowledge have been the concern of a diverse group of philosophers including Bergson, Gaston Bachelard, Martin Heidegger, Maurice Merleau-Ponty, Jean-Paul Sartre, Emmanuel Levinas, Elizabeth Grosz, Judith Butler and Paul Virilio, and some of these will reappear in later discussions.

In order to argue against idealist or transcendental reason, these scholars for the most part question the notion of an objective reality that is without some perspective on what it is to be subjective. By rejecting objective social or psychological explanations of human conduct, they seek to explain both the ontological aspects of our reality, its lived human-centeredness, as well as how that relates to the epistemological (historical and discursive) constitution of knowledge. Hence, phenomenologists may contrast representational or geometric space with the embodied experience of intelligible space and thus reflect upon the ways bodies move in the world. Applying this insight to theatre, Bert O. States contrasts the significative with the phenomenal as a mode of analysis by suggesting they may be called the 'useful' and 'delightful'. Usefulness, he suggests, 'implies a theatre image's transitivity, its sign-ness, or convertability into social, moral, or educational energy; whereas delight implies its "corporeality" and the immediate absorption of the image by the senses' (1985: 10). A dramatic text is not therefore a preconceived representation of characters and situations but, rather, a transitive phenomenological event, something waiting to happen, and about to be given form in the experience of performers and spectators.

Following from Bergson, Merleau-Ponty suggests that the sense of self is not directed from an inner motivating desire or an objective determination of action but instead emerges from the experience of the body moving towards, and with, things around it. The agency that we associate with human movement thus becomes enfolded in the experience of our senses, and the habits we form in relation to our environment, which at the same time become incorporated (through perception, attention and imagination) into our knowledge of the world. An often-cited mantra from Merleau-Ponty is that 'movements in themselves' never occur (2004: 115). For each individual every movement is, indissolubly, both movement and consciousness of movement since the movement and its background are 'moments of a unique totality' (2004: 122). I liken this to the feeling of walking in a strong wind, where one's steps progress the weight of the body but the skin is aware of the pressure of the air across the surface of the facing direction. The background atmosphere is not a representation associated or linked externally with corporeal movement but is immanent in the movement itself, inspiring and sustaining it at every moment. This emphasis on what is immanent suggests that any movement is never pure abstraction (that is, for some ideal purpose) unless it has a history in the experience of the body. Nor do we move without intentionality (as impulse or instinct alone, thus purely physiologically) since we move into our interactions with the world responsively. 'A movement is learned', writes Merleau-Ponty, 'when the body has understood it, that is, when it has incorporated it into its "world", and to move one's body is to aim at things through it; it is to allow oneself to respond to their call, which is made upon it independently of any representation' (2004: 123).

Hence, as we learn to move, even to 'play-act', we acquire consciousness of imitating a gesture or being able to dance within a repertoire of habituated motor coordination, and we also inhabit and enrich the scope of our experience in and of the world around us. Such orientation, while ontological, becomes a kind of existential knowing revealed through sensory perceptions but habituated and remembered in the body as a movement towards something in the world:

As soon as there is consciousness, and in order that there may be consciousness, there must be something to be conscious of, an intentional object, and consciousness moves towards this object only to the extent that it 'derealizes' itself and throws itself into it, only if it is wholly in this reference to ... something, only if it is a pure meaning-giving act. If a being is consciousness, he must be nothing but a network of intentions.

(Merleau-Ponty 2004: 114)

The feminist Iris Marion Young, writing in the latter part of the twentieth century, provides a powerful critique of the lack of sexual difference in these ideas about consciousness; that is, she suggests that who or what we are conscious of being, which is gendered, may influence our capacity to assert meaningful action. Her anthologized essay 'Throwing like a Girl' suggests that young women are not encouraged to experience, or achieve, the directness of purpose and aim in their 'gross movements' as much as young boys (1990: 143). Because socialized attributes of gender harness strength, position and weight in different ways, bodies will vary in the extent to which they can 'throw' themselves into worldly experience. Perhaps by extension, other kinds of difference are also limited by the theory of intentionality, where abstract intentional thought was assumed to determine the capacity for world-making. Such a claim has been contested now by more pluralistic and queer notions of bodybuilding, female sports and performativity, such as Butler proposed in Section One, which mess up binary notions of gender; however, Young's challenge to the abstract universals of phenomenology remains an important intervention.

Theatre scholar Stanton Garner provides sensitive readings of contemporary dramatic texts as if they are phenomenological worlds, arguing that the feminist plays of Caryl Churchill instantiate 'embodied, world-producing elements' (1994: 144) and he accepts Young's challenge that female corporeality needs to be staged as a 'body-in-movement' (1994: 206–7). In Churchill's *Top Girls*, for instance, six women from different historical periods assemble for a dinner party, setting the scene for encounters between their differently embodied worlds – compare the contrast between Isabella, the adventurous nineteenth-century traveller, and Nijo, a thirteenth-century Japanese courtesan. In a sense, the script provides an opportunity to explore how 'a network of intentions' shapes these characters; for Isabella, an attraction to 'manual work. Cooking, washing, mending, riding horses' or, for Nijo, the pleasure of a life 'being the Emperor's favourite and wearing thin silk' (2008: 4). Such learned and habituated movements condition their phenomenological experience of being gendered female, providing ample scope for theatrical experimentation with objects in rehearsal, and highlight the complexity of unravelling gendered experience from its entanglement with the world around it. As a theory for theatre, the phenomenological approach is therefore expansive in conceiving of the interplay between movement vitality and conscious identity.

Such a conception of the body-self recognizes that we are always in movement and shaped by movements folded by and into the world. According to Merleau-Ponty again, the analysis of subjective experience is

> subtended by an 'intentional arc' which projects round about us our past, our future, our human setting, our physical, ideological or moral situation, or rather which results in our being situated in all these respects. It is this intentional arc which brings about the unity of the senses, or intelligence, of sensibility and motility.
>
> (Merleau-Ponty 2004: 120–1)

In movement, with intentionality part of an arc towards knowing where we are situated, this proposition hovers around the extent to which motility, the freedom of movement and corporeal vitality remain fixed by external conditions or motivated from within; this external-internal dialectic of movement orientation and agency will complicate the research practices of theatre throughout the twentieth century as we will see in what follows.

Plasticity: Stanislavski

Having introduced the notion of movement vitality, let us return however to Delsarte's influence on modern theatre. I have explained that Delsarte's methods shaped the 'expression' of 'attitudes'; however, his approach was particularly formative in physical training systems because of its methods for developing kinaesthetic awareness: 'Repeatedly isolating each body part and then moving successionally through them, the practitioner developed a strong connection to gravity and a sense of movement as tensile and three-dimensional' (Foster 2011: 109). This simultaneous isolation, focus and expansion of movement repertoire within the body become critical to the concept of plasticity, observed at Hellerau and formally adopted as a core principle in actor training systems.

Plasticity as an attribute of a material substance is fluid and malleable, as well as durable. The plasticity of the actor, or in sculpture, means the body can change shape and be moulded, either in response to an external suggestion or with an inner impulse. Plasticity was to become therefore a method for experimenting with rhythmic iteration and corporeal transformation. To be plastic, or show plasticity, it might be argued, was to enhance the elastic nature of muscles and sinews in giving shape to character. Historically, the idea of plasticity emerges from the more static conception of showing expressive attitudes that was associated with the nineteenth-century genre of 'posing' in which actors would adopt the shape of a classical statue or portray a myth from a medieval frieze.

In *Modernism's Mythic Pose* (2011), Carrie Preston describes how the public and domestic entertainment of these 'poses plastiques' became incorporated into more scientific approaches to moral and physical spirituality but as importantly, the embodiment of the frozen gesture came to influence the aesthetics of theatre, cinema and modern poetry. Holding the pose may have been a way to communicate attitudes and ideals paired with poetry or music, as we saw with Delsarte and Craig, but the syncopation of bodily rhythms between the poses enabled the connection between gesture and expression to supplement metaphysical concepts with the material dimensions of a transitive state: neither one nor the other, the nymph could metamorphose into the lion, the angry gesture into the embrace. Such uncanny aspects of 'still motion' became critical to the effects of montage in early cinema – cutting from image to image with the audience able to grasp that an attitude could be held in suspense or contrast. Hence, poses were not just showing an idealized image of the body as a plastic medium but facilitating observation of both stasis and motion with subtle alignments that could expand the performance of dramatic character.

According to theatre scholar Rose Whyman, modern theatre directors were also keen to assert that theatre could be 'based on a scientific foundation ... on laws governing the sequence and alternation of movement'; hence, since the Moscow Art Theatre was exposed to Delsartean methods and other scientific ideas such as the Linnaen classification of nature into species and families or Darwin's ideas about the evolution of human expression, these concepts became relevant to their actor training. With his collaborator Sergei Volkonsky, a proponent of Dalcroze Eurhythmics, Stanislavski understood that the preparation of a modern actor would need a system of study that could transcend mere imitation and physical exertion if it was to communicate modern values and experience, so what became known as Stanislavski's 'System of Acting' had to be capable of producing positions, attitudes, strength, pace, direction, rhythm and gestural harmonies (Whyman 2008: 124).

In Stanislavski's manual *Building a Character* (1950), a key chapter focuses on the 'plasticity of motion', which is not, he suggests, just fluency nor the sentimental posing that is 'vacant and unintelligent' but rather requires the actor to develop their use of energy. Stanislavski writes: 'Energy, heated by emotion, charged with will, directed by the intellect, moves with confidence and pride, like an ambassador on an important mission. It manifests itself in conscious action, full of feeling, content and purpose ... it moves not only along your arms, your spine, your neck but also along your legs' (1950: 50). In a passage describing a 'plastic movement' class, the student-interlocutor Tortsov discusses how the actor might craft the art of walking, by skimming the ground and using tension in the spine to roll through the toes: 'no slowing down in the motion of the body as a step is taken' (58). Stanislavski instructs the actors to 'follow an inner pattern' as well as to 'draw physical attention to the movement of energy along a network of muscles' (61–3). Learning all the requisite preparatory skills such as gymnastics, ballet, fencing, stage fighting and acrobatics, the students will become physically energetic and decisive, but they must also develop a repertoire of images to inform and coordinate movements from the inner imagination – 'a spool of cotton, a ball of mercury, an outboard motor, the neck of a swan' – to name but a few (62–9). Any interruption of the flow of energy in realizing these inner motions will result in the disappointment of a 'motionless pose' and the stop-motion of an 'arrested action'. Plasticity rather than stasis is therefore generated by 'this inner feeling of energy passing through the body we call the sense of movement' (70). For Stanislavski, the understanding of action in character study was always underpinned by plasticity, and these new acting methods were dependent upon this unique convergence between attitude-posing, scientific knowledge and the emerging secular belief in psychological individuals rather than hereditary destiny.

What remains resilient in Stanislavski's thinking about the actor is the notion that the creative work of theatre will include an 'organic' aspect, whereby attentiveness to the 'natural force of gravity' carries the plot, while ensemble acting demands respect for the 'laws of nature' (Jones 1986: 75). Contradictions between the externally prepared physical apparatus of the body and voice must therefore mesh with the delicate inner life of the subconscious if theatre is not to 'violate nature' as its detractors in a secular age might contend. The paradox of a hidden structure of feeling in the 'subtext', which has been regarded as the key to naturalist dramatic writing, resonates then with the phenomenal qualities of movement – 'a web of innumerable, varied inner patterns' that are 'woven from "magic ifs", given circumstances, all sorts of figments of the imagination, inner movements [plasticity], objects of attention' (Jones 1986: 76). And the rhythmic patterning of speech and actions created in rehearsal will unfold with other objects, lighting and effects such as the twitching of buttons, pulling at skirts, picking up and putting down of glasses or guns. These phenomena become interpreted physically as movement-images revealing character, but they are also material things that invoke the imprecisions and acute sensations of memory.

Analysing Stanislavski's ground-breaking production of Anton Chekhov's *The Seagull* (1898), the theatre scholar David Richard Jones shows how the play's 'through-line' was given powerful affective and spiritual content by his annotation for the movement 'blocking' of the characters, Nina and Konstantin, in the 'climatic scene'.

> They spoke near the stove at right, where she went after flitting about the room. When she suggested that they sit and talk, they moved down right ... [later] according to Chekhov, 'Nina quickly puts on her hat and cloak.' Stanislavsky imagined her running 'across the whole length of the stage to the French window' with Konstantin in pursuit and then putting on her wrap. ... Before saying 'Sh-sh – I'm going!' she jumped up and came down again to the French windows ... After her departure, he (Konstantin) lingered there with the glass still in his hand.
>
> (Jones 1986: 68–9)

What is suggestive about this account of Stanislavski's dramaturgy is the sense of instability – flitting, running, jumping, lingering – that exists between these two fragile characters, and the agitating of an anticipated loss rendered so poignant in Nina's fleeting departure. Jones observes that '[e]xcept for these directions for physical movements, Stanislavsky said very little about this scene'; yet the choreography of these gestures – their motility and orientation in space, the pacing of stops and flowing actions – does render something 'comprehensible' (Jones 1986: 73). The progression of the play thus follows from apprehension, in relation to the feeling qualities of mood and tonality, and only later to 'comprehension' of the action.

For Jones, Stanislavski's theatrical innovation relates closely to this focus on the energies of movement study in which 'dialogues were subsumed in physical tasks as they are in our everyday existence' (74). What is known as naturalistic acting – which involves motive, utterance, movement and meaning – must produce the depiction of volatile emotional reality alongside the detailed history and intentionality of character. Such plasticity, the malleability of muscles and inner harmonies, within the formal logic of a scene is that which produces the effects of realism in Chekhov's plays, the entropy and falling apart of known worlds – as much as it does the powerful illusion of character in productions of the Moscow Art Theatre.

Case Study #2: *Hedda Gabler* (2005)

To bring these debates about posing, plasticity and naturalism into the present, let us look for a moment at German director Thomas Ostermeier's proto-cinematic production of Henrik Ibsen's *Hedda Gabler* (2005), developed with film-maker, Sébastien Dupouey, and stage designer, Jan Pappelbaum, and performed by actors from Berlin's Schaubühne. Regarded as a postdramatic director, Ostermeier's approach might suggest rejection of stage naturalism; however, it is oddly close to that of Stanislavski, since in Ostermeier's words, building a character still requires an actor who can be 'perceptive and alert to the manifestations of human action and human behaviour that surround him or her: how the body, gestures, how language changes, and how people adapt to different situations [including power relations] ... and how situations have a different effect on people's behaviour' (Boenisch and Ostermeier 2016: 23). Part of the repertoire that these Schaubühne actors bring to their construction of the mise en scène lies in the plasticity of a sophisticated movement vocabulary able to choreograph the adaptive behaviours of ambition and dislocated desire that so determine the plot.

Ostermeier's staging of this *Hedda Gabler* dismantles the embellishments of a naturalized nineteenth-century drawing room in favour of a more clinical atmosphere, with a revolving stage, glass walls and severely modernist furniture. Integrating film (stills, close-ups, time-loops) into the performance, observations of self and other are acutely entangled by shadowy reflections in the glass and a transparency between on- and offstage action. The actors perform with quasi-banal, and certainly understated, realist actions such as putting on slippers, clipping flowers, reading the computer or sticking post-it notes on the wall. But these actions alternate with stylized movements, such as the slowing down of a sideways glance and silhouetted poses that communicate an attitude, such as contempt or anxiety, if not a state of mind. The actor playing Hedda is almost continuously on stage, often just held in suspense, her gaze cool, swallowing a little, with a half-smile. This pause forms a critical aspect of the plasticity of action; it reveals the shift that must take place between one situation and another. Audience attention is thus arrested by the difficulty of linking narrative cause and effect, because each tableau-vivant stages the possibility of a contrasting point of view. At the midway point of the play, which opens Act Three, the two women are asleep on the L-shaped sofa, but Hedda's neat semi-foetal body at one end contrasts with the straight, yet slumped body of Thea Elvstedt – this scene of their unconscious selves hence exposes their intimacy and estrangement at one and the same time.

Let us look in more detail at the pivotal moment in Act Three, in which Hedda destroys Lövborg's manuscript. When the boyish actor, Katharina Schüttler, playing Hedda recovers Lövborg's computer hidden under the couch, she nurses it for some time as if it is a treasured relic, or the stolen or lost child that Thea believes it is, but she does not display any apparent curiosity about its contents. A character-based interpretation might say this shows the superficiality of Hedda's mind, but she is in a sense holding the pose, arresting the malevolence of her intentionality. The production gives her ample time in between scenes to immerse herself in reading the machine, lowering the lights and leaving her within the glow of flickering images of men, trees, houses and water that play on the screens. Later when she wields the hammer there is no mistaking the plasticity, or mutability, of her move towards assertive defiance. Once the arm is lifted, she pauses to look around and confirm not that she is alone or unobserved but as if she, taking up a partly psychological and partly symbolic attitude, wants to witness herself as the producer of the action. Decisive and no longer a victim, she becomes one of the Furies, the perpetrator of retribution – smash, smash, smash – as the audience watches the computer shatter, splintering keys, metal and plastic into the darkness before the stage revolves.

Hedda's self-destructiveness has often shocked audiences, but the first actresses in the role, such as Elizabeth Robbins in the late nineteenth century, also portrayed the opposing affect by revealing Hedda's own sense of horror (Cima 1993: 49–51). Perhaps a contemporary audience used to stories of domestic violence can more easily imagine how a bourgeois woman may act violently in an untenable domestic situation. For Ostermeier, however, it was not Hedda's vengeance but 'the boredom' that he wanted to articulate: 'It expresses itself in a different tone, in different movements, in different manners of physicality' (Boenisch and Ostermeier 2016: 23). For this expression, Schüttler spends much of the play resisting interaction, pulling away from Hedda's husband Tesman, resisting the crude advances of Judge Brack and tauntingly distant from Lövborg's outbursts. And yet the realization of Hedda's character is not produced by the violent excess of gesture but visible in these small and particular constrictions that pin her to their desires. This plasticity of the actor works through the fibres of her body and manifests the psychological terror of Hedda's entrapment.

We do not know when patterns of habit will produce and trigger certain actions. Her intention – and the traditional motivations of a naturalist actor – seems inscrutable although the critical choice the character makes as a woman and as a wife exists in the gaps. In this sense, Hedda gesturing with the gun seems to be only an ambiguous pretence, part of her 'act', because holding the gun becomes the familiar movement around which the play pivots. In the transmission of the pistol to Lövborg, she presses it into his hands as a love gift and it is in asking him to suicide that her agency is most pronounced. In the Ostermeier production, she embraces the blood-spattered Lövborg but he twitches like little more than a scarecrow. She steps back and her immaculate white collar is unstained, so the action of embrace denies the reality of the situation, which is her drive for violence. The gun's final reversal as a weapon in Hedda's hands is still destined to traumatize the spectator, and rather than conclude with the script's discovery of her body, this production montages the bloodied Hedda lying crumpled on the adjacent, visible outer wall with the characters Tesman, Mrs Elvsted and Judge Brack chatting together in the living room.

The palpable tensions of a gendered aggression that can snap at any time are visible in the movement plasticity – Hedda's angular leaning on a wall or Tesman grabbing her wrists to shake her. And it is in this sense that the Ostermeier production remains a form of heightened naturalism much like Nordic noir TV drama. In close-ups by the camera lens, as with Henry Irving's face, the audience is always conscious of Schüttler's visage reflected through the glass: Hedda becomes the flickering image of motility, lit and darkening, cheeks pale, eyes darting, and slight breath of fear in and out. Under the lights, the subtle movements of her body appear as a moth to the flame, reanimating the experiments of modern drama – by utilizing the techniques of *poses plastiques*, montage and modern dance. The phenomenological, that is everything in the world around the character, folds into the power of movement perception to register new ideas and emotions.

For Stanislavski and the naturalist playwrights, as much as for contemporary directors such as Ostermeier, the theatre of modern drama invites the testing of human consciousness as impulses, intentions and hesitations, which are movement responsive to the felt aspects, the mood qualities, of a phenomenal world as well as much as its social coordinates. We are moved by what surrounds us, and we in turn move towards, or are restrained by, that which we desire from our relations with others. This phenomenological world view was historically, and of necessity, always in dialogue with other models of human movement potential, such as we will see in the following discussions of Meyerhold and Brecht.

Mechanics: Meyerhold

Building on the bodily plasticity of the actor, the theatre becomes increasingly concerned with how to organize the assemblage of movement in relation to changing social conditions and new technologies of motion. In the introduction to Section Two, I foregrounded modern artistic fascination with the moving image in cinema, poetry and visual art, and art movements such as futurism and vorticism had movement as defining ideas. Propelling the study of motion were the photographic experiments of Eadweard Muybridge which asserted that animal motion was mechanical in design and could support scientific segmentation of the functioning of the biophysical organism.

Asked by the American transport baron Leland Stanford in 1878 to determine how a horse runs at full gallop –

whether with alternating or straight legs fully suspended or not – Muybridge, after a series of experiments, placed along a track a series of large cameras that were to be triggered by a thread as the horse passed. Then projecting these still images as a sliding sequence through a viewing machine called a Zoopraxiscope, also invented by Muybridge, the slightly jerky effect gave the impression of the horse in continuous motion, proving that the legs become synchronized inwards and, yes, remain in the air. Muybridge's dry-plate photographs later published as *The Human Figure in Motion* (1955) extended his findings about the mediated perception of stillness and motion to people walking, carrying objects and working. One sequence of a young woman trailing a scarf and turning around creates the illusion of a three-dimensional body appearing and disappearing from view. As we find when dancing under a glitter ball, the suggestion of movement can be conveyed as the reception of different instants – a turn of the torso or flick of the wrist – a tantalizing sense of artistic effect. But the images also extended the metaphor of the human body as efficient machine because they showed how distributions of weight, the effects of gravity and the accurate delivery of a gesture could be studied as 'biomechanics'.

The coordination of bodily effort, so closely linked to how we displace weight, was a project designed to improve industrial productivity. The American engineer, Frederick Winslow Taylor, with his 1909 book *The Principles of Scientific Management* is credited with devising methods to measure 'time and motion' as a system guaranteeing movement efficiency with quantifiable uses of human energy allocated to specific tasks. American performance theorist Jon McKenzie (2001) has argued that the Taylorist efficiency of effort dominates discourses of movement from the mid-twentieth century in relation to 'improving performance' in the workplace, the military and competitive sports and hence that ideology is embedded in relations with capitalist production globally. Today, similar versions of movement science extend into everyday life with wearable activity trackers such as the Fitbit and exercise programmes such as Pilates designed to carefully target specific muscles. The reason for considering the influence of both Muybridge and Taylor in terms of theories of movement in theatre is that this segmentation of movement was to impact artists who wanted to radicalize theatre away from depictions of petty bourgeois existence and towards representation of the culture of machines, both industrial and human, in modern life.

After years of work as an actor with Stanislavski's Moscow Art Theatre, Vsevolod Meyerhold left in 1902 to establish his own career as a director of both classical and new plays during the fervent years of change in pre- and post-revolutionary Russia. This cosmopolitan scene of theatre artists, writers and critics created an intellectual milieu that encouraged publications, studios for theatre training and a vibrant exchange with a well-informed audience. Although Meyerhold and Stanislavski are often regarded as opposing figures, they occupied the same artistic landscape, and Meyerhold's vision of a 'theatre of the future' was regarded as a refreshing force, forging new ground with his experimental approach to production and questioning of approaches to character and dramatic form. By stripping away the curtains, clutter and props, and thrusting the stage forward into the auditorium, Meyerhold's constructivist theatre could exhibit the sculptural plasticity of his actors as episodic situations, and they could manipulate the dramaturgy of hitherto unrealized scenes such as parades, laments and protests that could speak to the emergent proletariat. Iconic photographs from his theatre show stages constructed of platforms, ladders and ramps upon which tensile figures are posed with flags or leaning heavily against rows of tables and chairs. A 2019 production of *Wozzeck* directed by William Kentridge at the Metropolitan Opera in New York owed much to the diagrams of scaffolding and stairs that form part of the Meyerhold aesthetic, and in this work the one stage design was rapidly transformed from urban street scapes to bar rooms to riverside scenes. The 'theatre of the future', argued Meyerhold in 1920, required both a technical transformation as well as a social revolution that would consist of 'plenty of light, plenty of high spirits, plenty of grandeur, plenty of infectious enthusiasm, unlaboured creativity, the participation of the audience in the corporate creative act of performance' (Braun 2016: 209).

For this new theatre, Meyerhold wanted to prepare the actor with the skilled movement of industrial production, and (following Taylor) he suggests 'the spectacle of a man working efficiently affords positive pleasure' (Braun 2016: 244). His actor training programme of 'biomechanics' aimed to reduce the superfluity of gestures to develop rhythm (following Dalcroze), to locate the body in relation to gravity (physical anatomy) and to improve stability (by understanding structure). Like Stanislavski, Meyerhold devised a series of training methods, or *études*, for actors to use in preparation for a role; however, his were unrelated to organic sentiment but would instead investigate the 'rhythmic, exact, plastic' components of an action (Rudnitsky, 1981: 327). The Meyerhold instructor, Nikolaus Wolcz, can be seen teaching two actors in an online video about how such 'acting chains' of 'intention, execution and reaction' should function (Schmidt 1996: 39). In 'Preparation of the dagger', they begin by pacing the stage, swinging their arms with sharpened elbows, face to face, and then, on a counted instruction, leap into a fixed pose. Like a runner on a starting block with their muscles tensed, the actors strike up a physical relation: one actor leans inwards to unsheathe an imaginary sword, which he plunges into the open chest of the other; the second actor folds back and then leans forwards, followed by a sudden backward collapse. Lying flat with arms outstretched, his stiffened body is lifted from behind by the dagger owner, who carries the 'corpse' until it falls and rolls to one side. At this sign of deadness, the sequence ends and the two actors run energetically side by side before leaving the stage.

The Meyerhold scholar Jonathan Pitches (2003) argues that the physical preparation of the body through activities, such as shifting weight or holding and playing with sticks that represent a multitude of props, can distort an attitude or define an intention to move which has wider political implications.

Even when an unexpected image was a 'reject' in rehearsal, Meyerhold would try to utilize

> a structured gesture to present a possibility, a virtuality, and idea. This is a social act. It involves two gestures; the primary one is the gesture of presentation: the act which indicates and defines the gesture as gesture and which demands from the spectator the gesture of response.
>
> (Schmidt 1996: xv)

The form of a gesture therefore becomes the unit *par excellence* in an actor's movement repertoire, since the gesture hails, or calls, the spectator. Interested in how popular theatre, such as the 'fairground booth', quickly establishes the details of a situation and its action, I would suggest that Meyerhold crafts the dagger movement phrase like a theatrical haiku. Distilled as an arc of gestural stop-motion, the performance can exhibit every variety of a murderous knife attack; since each component is punctuated by a clapping sound upon which the actors jump from action to action, the effect functions like a cinematic cut at the most intense moments of the scene. Repeated with strenuous effort – preparing and using a dagger – the situation expands as a sign. Without any commentary or portrayal of intention, the assemblage of these segmented images conjures the affective horror of the scene's violence without imitating the whole gory event.

In anticipation of Brecht's defamiliarizing of the everyday gesture to make an ideological point, Meyerhold's 'new approach' thrived on those aspects of the grotesque which 'parade[s] ugliness in order to prevent beauty from lapsing into sentimentality' (Braun 2016: 138). The 'ugliness' of a movement was not its continuity with familiar actions but its discontinuity of gesture, orientation and trajectory, as Meyerhold explains:

> What is basic to the grotesque is the progress of the viewer from one just-deciphered plane of perception into another, totally unexpected one. Then; any gesture, any step, any

turn of the head – in a word, any motion is examined as an element of dance, understood as it was in old Japanese theatre. I am most interested in clowns, their quick, rhythmic change from one movement to the next in unexpected leaps.
(Meyerhold cited in Rudnitsky 1981: 160)

The departure from realist theatre, as with many other modernist ideas, derived much from growing awareness of Asian theatre techniques with artists such as Meyerhold, Artaud and Grotowski all referencing tours of Japanese theatre, Balinese and Indian *kathak* dancers. In addition to the lure of exoticism and the problems of appropriation, in the performing arts, the codification of gesture in non-Western forms – such as we saw in Section One's discussion of the Natyasastra – confirms that a studied movement repertoire can convey dramatic and intensely affective narratives. In developing biomechanics, Meyerhold's ambition was to 'find forms and colours, movements and sounds, that symbolically would express the soul and content locked within the dramatic action' rather than reproducing a naturalist aesthetics (Rudnitsky 1981: 214). As much as Meyerhold was experimenting with the efficiencies of the body as a movement sign, he was also developing his approach to direction through a 'constructivist' stage choreography that we shall analyse in the following case study. This case study of *The Constant Prince* is in two parts with a contrasting version directed by Grotowski analysed later in relation to ecstatic movement.

Case Study #3, part a: *The Constant Prince* (1915)

Written in the seventeenth century by Spanish playwright Pedro Calderón, *The Constant Prince* is set in the fifteenth-century period of the Spanish inquisition, and it examines the crisis in religious belief felt by a Prince whose sense of military duty to his people lay in conflict with his pacificist preferences as a poet or scholar. Rarely performed today, because religious piety and humility seem to have little representation within the leadership of contemporary society, it was however a work that attracted both Meyerhold and Grotowski as theatre directors perhaps because of the religious and political contradictions they experienced in early-twentieth-century Russia, on the one hand, and post–Second World War Poland, on the other.

In Meyerhold's production of *The Constant Prince* staged at the Alexandrinsky Theatre in 1915, he notoriously had Prince Fernando performed as a travesty role, with a leading actress playing the male character, and rather than a faithful historical production, he projected the mise en scène forward to Calderón's time in order to expose the conflicts between Catholic religious authority and Spanish Moorish culture. For reasons that were no doubt more obvious to his audience, Meyerhold chose to explore the 'feminine faith' of the 'noble prince' although some critics saw this a trick that removed the heroic element from the Crusader's final acts of renunciation (Rudnitsky 1981: 215). Framing the palace chambers with an open proscenium stage, decorations were changed by 'the servants' under full view of the audience, with stylized colours, movements and sounds designed to convey the mood of the Spanish court. Under instruction, however, the actors 'moved forward slowly with cautious, calculated steps, as though walking a tightrope; or they froze in place, one leg behind, body leaning back, arms raised tensely', an effect, according to one reviewer, in which 'the nerves were teased by the extreme deliberateness' (1981: 215–16). One actor, perhaps exercising his biomechanic virtuosity, 'moved about the stage with nothing less than the leaps of a tiger' so that the St Petersburg audience seeking to appreciate the virtues of the Prince felt that the production was a travesty (1981: 216). Tapping into an animal nature of coiled resentment with these movements was bound to disrupt expectations, if only to expose the inner tensions, of a play about a contemplative religious life.

A 2014 workshop production of 'the fool' scene from Meyerhold's *The Constant Prince* prepared by Kuden Theatre in Berlin shows the performers wearing stage blacks and, as with the previous biomechanics training, running on the spot between each action, making the theatre resemble a sports session. Minus the historical context of Meyerhold's interpretation, that during the First World War in Europe (1914–18), one can barely sense the comedic tension that underlies the serious intent: however the actors strike threatening poses, change positions in response to a compelling beat and assail the fool Brito, who falls backwards in front of a mob. According to the Russian theatre historian Konstantin Rudnitsky, Meyerhold's *The Constant Prince* disturbed his critics because it transposed militaristic patriotism into the representation of simple and humble faith, making a virtue of qualities other than the 'steel' of powerful people (1981: 216). Discontinuities of character, ensemble and period in the production also anticipated much of Meyerhold's radical constructivist staging in his post-revolutionary RSFSR First Theatre in Moscow. From Meyerhold's theories, or rather the evidence of biomechanics and his experimental productions, we derive the notion that the demonstrable structure of gesture is a manifestation of the social in motion, rather than an expression of organic identity.

Dynamics: Laban

In their different approaches, both Stanislavski and Meyerhold developed the notion of plasticity – the embodied intentions to be discovered between the poses or attitudes held by the formations of character and social groups – but what was lacking in this theory was a more dynamic, or rhythmic, approach to movement variation. Dynamics in music produce the variation in the volume of sound, so dynamics in physical movement must produce qualitative variation in the emphasis given to gestures, attitudes and comportments within a scene. And this sense of dynamics is related in a significant way to how we understand what it is to do work or put effort into an activity. For an expanded conception of effort and dynamic variation we will turn now to Rudolf Laban before looking at the extension of effort analysis to the work of Bertolt Brecht.

Laban was an Hungarian choreographer and movement educator who worked in Germany and the UK and produced an influential body of movement theory in the mid-twentieth century. Following the tradition of both Delsarte and Dalcroze, Laban elaborated ideas about movement philosophy and analysis that extended into many fields. His book *The Mastery of Movement on the Stage* (1950, republished 2011) elaborates upon a range of movement concepts that can be applied to mime, acting or dance. The notion of the *kinesphere*, for instance, maps the extension of the body into surrounding space as a three-dimensional dynamo-sphere of potential movement; *eukinetics* is the study of rhythm while investigation of *space harmony* distributes the influence of weight, time and space across various planes; *trace-forms* are patterns that remain from movement pathways; and his system of *kinetography*, or Labanotation, graphically annotates choreography like a musical score. In terms of movement theory, however, one of his most influential fields of research is that of dynamics, a concept that transforms the energetic qualities of movement plasticity by recognizing the use of effort, or the distributed use of tension, to change the performance of a movement or action. Far from being simply a measure of efficiency, Paola Crespi explains that effort for Laban is both individual exertion and creative force combined: 'Individual effort is a force that, inflected by gestures, becomes rhythmical and, more generally, effort is the vital force or élan vital which in its rhythmical exertions and recuperations shapes reality as much as human (and non-human) action' (2014: 3). The use of polyrhythmic dynamics – through the application of effort – is what makes human, animal or machine interesting to watch, and Laban set out to scientifically study its core principles.

For Laban, the qualities of movement dynamics are shaped by three fundamental elements of motion – time, space and force – and these incorporate opposing factors so that time can be either quick or slow, space direct or indirect, and force (often linked with the uses of weight and gravity) weak or strong. The combination of these movement elements then produces eight dynamic qualities called 'efforts': gliding, floating, pressing, wringing, thrusting, slashing, dabbing and flicking. The Croatian dance educator Vera Maletić explains these kinetic qualities as the 'nucleation [assemblage]' of body parts or whole body patterns that 'arises, lasts, vanishes and generates' in the performance of an action (1987: 93). An example might be waving a hand, an action which can be done vigorously, with a strong energetic sense of flicking or thrusting the hand into the air, or alternatively presented as a slow wafting gesture, floating perhaps vaguely into the distance. Or with movement dynamics applied to a concrete situation, the waving gesture could begin strongly as a departing person leaves but fades away, gliding down the torso, as the friend disappears from view. The variation in the gesture reveals a qualitative application of movement effort which conveys attitude as well as situation. Being able to assemble the different aspects of a rising and falling dynamics, in Laban movement analysis terms, creates the intensification of movement qualities for performance. Notably, this dynamic oscillation resembles the Noh 'flower' that opens and fades (discussed in Section One) as a principle of the actor's craft.

Transforming the kinesphere into the dynamosphere, Laban also identified the labile properties of fluency or stability as integral to a formal study of movement. The flow of a gesture or action may vary from 'free or bound' in the kinesphere, which means effort can either 'indulge' or 'fight' (resist) the continuous delivery of the action. Returning to the vigorous wave or the wafting drooping hand from above, these labile dimensions can incrementally alter the 'inner attitudes' communicated by a performer. Applied to movement an inner attitude will vary expression in performance: harnessing effort to weight, for instance, becomes associated with 'Intending' and generates an attitude of 'Sensing', while the quality of flow is associated with 'Adapting' and the attitude of feeling. Combining 'weight and flow', the wave might seem 'dreamlike, or creative'; hence it has an 'Indulging' quality, or with more control, hence bound, the same gesture might seem 'doubting, or restrictive' (hence resistant) towards embodiment of the relationality of a farewell. As Maletić writes, 'the naming and isolation of these elements one from the other thus gave actors an opportunity to develop a movement vocabulary that might be independent of emotion, or character, and yet inform the shaping and rhythm of a production, scene by scene' (1987: 101). We will apply selected aspects of Laban's movement analysis of scenic dynamics to an extended case study of Brecht's production of *Mother Courage* but let's first consider some of Brecht's own ideas about movement in theatre.

Arrangement: Brecht

Bertolt Brecht was a playwright, director and Marxist intellectual in mid-century Germany, although for some part of his career he made works in the United States. His many famous plays (*Man Equals Man*, *The Caucasian Chalk Circle* or *Galileo*, mentioned earlier) are regularly performed, in translation and around the world, because they examine so many concepts of what realism is able to represent in the theatre. Brecht's conception of defamiliarization (*Verfremdung*), making a familiar action or situation seem strange or 'alienated', has been a focus of much contemporary theatre studies. Close examination of productions directed by Brecht shows he had a finely tuned approach to movement dramaturgy: 'Divide up the actor's part and modulate it, thoroughly savouring it, until it suits him. He must "arrange" his movements, whatever they are meant to express, in such a way that he gets fun out of their sweep and rhythm' (Brecht 1978: 243). While the political intent is clear, there was nothing dull, or too earnest, about this process, and Brecht makes clear that the pleasure of movement, its 'sweep and rhythm' were central to his interest in theatrical expression. Movement dynamics were also essential for understanding the operations of 'fate' in preparation of the plot and its dramaturgy.

Brecht however rejected abstracted movement exercises or 'warm-ups' for corporeal plasticity, preferring to begin his rehearsals with detailed and lengthy discussion of the text. Not unlike Meyerhold, the task of rehearsal was to understand how each situation dramatizes a specific social condition, so the precise blocking of scenes with realistic gestures was his next phase. Some of his productions are documented with 'model books' (*modelbuch*) which include annotated photographs of each scene and notes which explain that 'the grouping and movement of the characters has to narrate the story, which is a chain of incidents' (Jones 1986: 90). Carl Weber, who became the director of the Berliner Ensemble after Brecht, expands further on how these groupings were developed in a 1989 BBC interview: '[W]e try 20 or 30 different variations of every scene, moving the people in the scene, of grouping the people ... to get an "arrangement", as we call it in German, or plotting which tells the story by itself'. Constructed like a sharply moving tableau, the 'chain of incidents' will also include any interruptions to the movement flow that allow the spectator to realize their response to the contradictions between character and story.

The *Couragemodell* for his 1949 production of *Mother Courage* expands upon this idea of positioning the actors as the first phase of activating the play. While such a static conception seems antithetical to movement exploration, finding a way to shift from one still frame to another – recalling the stop-motion images of Muybridge – releases attention to what a micro-movement can show. Think of the difference between open hands that are facing upwards or facing down or, even more minimally, a turning of the thumbs in an open hand. Ironically, by restricting movement, Brecht enhances the justification for visibilizing movement intent:

> Positions should be retained as long as there is no compelling reason for changing them: and a desire for variety is not a compelling reason. If one gives in to a desire for variety, the consequence is a devaluation of all movement on the stage; the spectator ceases to look for a specific meaning behind each movement, he stops taking movement seriously.
>
> (Brecht cited in Jones 1986: 90)

Movement study becomes thus a determined work of stage business, and Brecht's concentration was on how movement details were constructed in partnership with the actor so that actions were instructive and entertaining, hence dialectical or 'gestic'. The point that feminist theatre scholars such as Elin Diamond (1988) have made is that gestic movements foreground corporeal iconicity (the desire for resemblance) and historicize action, rendering them as 'A-effects', or alienation effects, that form aspects of a 'moving dialectic': 'The crux of "historicization" is change: through A-effects spectators observe the potential movement in class relations, discover the limitations and strengths of their own perceptions, and begin to change their lives' (Diamond 1988: 87). Such physical examples of gender and class dynamics are not then dissolved into motivations of character which would obscure and 'naturalize' them, but rather they are held up to view as a commentary on social conditions. The more specific the gesture or movement in a stage scene, the greater the likelihood that there will be 'points of astonishment' for the audience – a concept that might add to what we think of as defamiliarization – astonishment suggesting the affects of shock, bafflement and wonder. The alienation of a movement sign – registering as emotional, psychological and physical – therefore represents more than an intellectual understanding of the contradictions inherent in the drama.

Case Study #4: *Mother Courage and Her Children* (1949, 2006)

By way of expanding Brecht's contribution to movement theory, I will examine the actress Helene Weigel's expressive comportment in the original 1949 Berliner Ensemble production of *Mother Courage* and contrast it, more briefly, with the 2006 rendition by the actress Meryl Streep. Scarf pulled over her brow, Mother Courage, bent double and harnessed to her cart, is one of the great movement 'arrangements' of twentieth-century theatre, and many aspects of Weigel's gestic acting in that role have been analysed, such as the open-mouthed 'silent scream' or the way in which she counts out money and bites the coin to ensure that it is not counterfeit (Jones 1986: 120–1).

A different example of gestic astonishment, whereby movement becomes a sign of difference, occurs in *Mother Courage* after the body of Courage's daughter Kattrin has been taken away for burial and when the inevitably destructive path of war seems most profound. At this moment in her performance, Weigel as Courage slows down the action instead of bringing the performance of the scene to its sad ending. First, she splices her walking stick so that the rope will not slip when she pulls the cart alone. In a very real sense this action binds her to the cart – the burden of war that she carries – but it is also her prosthetic instrument for the work of the future. She leans forward, slightly to her right, so that the rope falls behind and over the right shoulder, taking time to hitch up her scapula and lean again to tauten the rope. The cart is more than her body weight so she must use her body as a lever to inch it forward across the stage. As with corporeal mime, what is absent rather than present in the effort of movement becomes apparent: the horse or bullock that might have pulled the cart; the two strong sons who did pull the cart; and finally, the daughter with whom Courage had previously shared the load. Since the cart represents home and workplace, mobile dwelling and business proposition, Courage is now isolated with the material conditions of her fate: 'every gesture signifies a decision' (Brecht 1978: 69). Weigel tugs and then slightly stumbles, as she drags the cart several times around the stage. Brecht intended this rotation to activate the audience – 'when it goes on rolling there is a moment of irritation ("this has been going on long enough"). But when it goes on still longer, a deeper understanding sets in' (Brecht, cited in Jones 1986: 125). As a movement image the rolling propels an affective response. And rather than the performance of smooth, harmonious movement, what Lefebvre and Laban call eurhythmy, Weigel's jolting motion exemplifies kakorythmy, a phenomenon of movement that is disordered, 'catapulted from extreme to extreme' even to the perception or impression of 'distress' (Laban, 2014: 76–7).

In addition to consideration of gestic movement, a Laban effort analysis would analyse motility; that is how rhythmic momentum shapes the tragic dialectics of this production. Theatre often glosses movements such as walking which reveal the ordinary aspects of an individual's story, but as Weigel observes in the BBC interview: 'People are intelligent, and looking at plays that are also intelligent, they understand too that it is not destiny, deity or kings who have absolute power to change their life. Looking at small people, like we do, like we play them in our theatre, maybe they learn to behave like thinking human beings.' How one walks, as we've considered in the introduction, together with how the rhythm of walking communicates, is a reasonable question to ask of Brecht's theatre. In this play about a woman surviving the durational impact of war, the topography of marching (as the emphatic military variant of walking) provides, I would suggest, a movement structure that connects all scenes in the play.

Let us analyse how Mauss's 'techniques of the body' (discussed in this book's Introduction) result in energetic transpositions across the stage. Brecht himself writes of asking actors to 'transpose' their movements into that of third-person past tense, which is something habituated as subjective knowledge but seen objectively. For my part I am interested in how such temporal transpositions are highlighted by changes in spatial comportment and effort dynamics. Laban's concept of an expanded 'kinesphere' has produced 'trace-forms', or movement memories, that have been indelibly registered by the work of Weigel's moving body in this iconic production.

When the play opens and the carriage rolls into view, Courage strides like a man, takes large steps and keeps up a steady beat. In Laban's terms, her efforts through the feet and legs are direct, strong and quick – and as such she conveys a 'punching' attitude that is bold, crass and rude. The folding or swinging of Courage's wide skirt also communicates the labile, adaptive states of Courage's mind – resolve, attack and cunning – and thus participates in the dialectical consciousness that is to be provoked in the audience. With weight rolling through the feet her dynamosphere is 'Intending' and expands with a confidence that extrudes outwards and forwards into the open stage. In this early scene, the noises of war beckon and she is excited by the fortunes it may bring her and her family, and Brecht's blocking contrasts the relatively static positioning of the Recruiting Officer and Sergeant, with the animation of Mother Courage and her children, even passing the Sergeant's helmet around as a kind of game. The forceful gaiety of this 'arrangement' is soon changed when she loses her first son to the war machine, and her steady walking appears suddenly blocked: 'Mother Courage stands quite still, then,' instructs Brecht (1962: 12). The phrasing of this stage direction emphasizes the actor's awareness of arrested motion in order that the character 'achieves the A-effect by being seen to observe his own movement' (Brecht 1978: 71).

Oddly, Brecht's notes on the play convey little about the pace of each scene, although precise timings exist for the intervals between scenes and the production's overall duration. Perhaps this omission results from his trust in familiar actors, for which an agreed choreographed metre marked the social habitus, or shared understandings and practices of the ensemble, and their acquired 'techniques'. Mauss notes, for instance, the distinctive 'goose step' – outstretched legs moving at a brisk pace – which was a recognized part of Nazi marching action but there is also the social solidarity of children marching to school or swinging along in recreational settings, such as a hike in the woods. Courage's first march seems to be a bouncy variation on the goose step, and its rhythmic action kicks up her skirt. She is joyful in these efforts of keeping pace and being in tune with the business and movement of war. In Scene Four, the 'Song of the Great Capitulation' ironizes the normalization of marching in a war zone and makes explicit how the pace of marching contributes to the rhythmic dialectics of the performance:

> The bird says: Wait a year or so
> And marching with the band we go
> Keeping in step, now fast now slow
> And piping out our little spiel.
> Then one day the battalions wheel
> And we go down upon our knees
> To God Almighty if you please.

> (Brecht 1962: 44)

By way of contrast in the final Scene Twelve, Courage is alone and her marching becomes jerky; she staggers forward, still quite strong, but indirect – in Laban's terms, the effort equates to 'wringing', depending on the amount of weight twisted behind each gesture. Since the action-drive is bound to the cart and is not free-flowing, her kinesphere falls lower to the ground and the movement intentions are focused on 'Sensing', like an animal cowering, or scurrying for cover. With her eyes nearly closed, these final movements of Courage do not convey an inner mental state or a static position in relation to preceding events; rather, Weigel, the actor, shows the spectators a figure bound to the continuous production of bodily effort in keeping alive.

The dialectic, then, of an 'animal endurance and ability to bear burdens' was embodied in these movements designed to affect audience members, including critics such as Roland Barthes and Bernard Dort who were profoundly affected by this first production, with Barthes stressing the intensity of 'edification mixed with delight' and Dort at a loss for words with the power of its 'fragmented present' (cited in Fensham 2019: 54).

In 2006, a unique collaboration between playwright Tony Kushner and leading actress Meryl Streep, directed by George C. Wolfe, transformed this iconic historical rendition of *Mother Courage* into a new genre of political theatre for the Delacorte open air theatre in Central Park New York. With a backdrop of current US involvement in the Iraq war, the idea of women carrying the burden of feeding the army and burying the bodies of young people was not far from the reality. With Streep playing Courage dressed in jungle greens, she describes her role as forming 'the lost songs ... of dead people'. The translation – in musical and corporeal terms – of the Song of the Great Capitulation is a brilliantly transposed 'arrangement' of its rhythmic dialectics. It drops the marching analogy and refers to the rhythm more colloquially as 'when push comes to shove', an almost perfect description of 'effort' itself. Leaning on a step Streep removes her shoes, while Courage reflects upon the 'perverted courage' of the poor, 'who carry the weight of the wealthy on their broad, stupid backs' (recorded in the 2008 documentary, *Theater of War)*. With a voice that contrasts coarse recitative with a light melodic tone, Streep frowns and waves her hands – dividing up and modulating her part as Brecht instructed – as if caught between one emotion and another. Weight – the carrying of the cart – and flight – the imaginary bird that might seem to offer freedom – are juxtaposed thus in the song and the gestic movements of the performance. Updated to the twenty-first century, the feeling of time, space and force that meaningless work demands in the theatre of war, in Brecht's terms, produces minimal consciousness of its own oppression, and Courage does not seek pity. Instead, the audience must identify their own knowledge of exploited, wasted and disastrous effort in situations that reduce human beings to mere remains. As Streep explains in the documentary, it might be the horror of war that we try to remember but for women it is the 'why? that is cried over the body of their children'.

Philosophically, the rhythmic movement of Mother Courage scores and notates the long history of war and military occupation in the lived experience of ordinary people. Why, one might ask, in terms of theatre, study the way in which a single actor interprets the role of Mother Courage through movement? If, as I'm suggesting, Weigel and then Streep are making theatre represent the reality of bodies marked by history, violence and work, then such close observation of techniques of the body, and their movement qualities, enables an aesthetic dynamics that can become the focus of critical attention and political dialectics. The difference between a Laban and a Brechtian analysis may however depend upon the extent to which individual actors can unlearn or de-habituate their participation in regulated systems and corporeal techniques in order to better reveal or change social forces and situations.

Somatics: Grotowski

If theorists of dramatic form became concerned with rejecting the scope of movement as energetic or forward momentum, an opposite path emerged from the journey in theatre production towards states of altered consciousness through *ekstasis*, or the ecstatic. A lineage of twentieth-century theatre directors that includes Antonin Artaud and Jerzy Grotowski sought to expand the intensified experience of the moving body to its limits and to re-ritualize theatre through trance-like performance practices. Unlike the approaches of Stanislavski, Meyerhold and Brecht –

which assumed the value of harnessing movement for theatre, by turning the forces operating on and through the body into productive, political and artistic communication – many artists and theorists regard with suspicion the potential of systems to create a theatre which might rehabilitate the abjection of the human in contemporary society. For them, the modernist 'will to power' has failed, and in the contemporary European context, the heirs of Artaud are those working in the 'theatre of images' such as Teatro Raffaello Sanzio (Kelleher 2015); with 'the power of theatrical madness' such as Jan Fabre (productions in 1984 and 2013); or the 'theatre of deconstruction' with the Japanese company, Gekidan Kaitaisha (Broinowski 2017).

Some of this rejection of European modernism and scientific progress participates in a post-imperial fascination with what can be recovered from that which is ungoverned or unregulated. This form of movement theory is often linked to Nietzsche's revaluation of the Dionysiac role of ritual theatre in ancient Greek culture. In his 1872 book, *On the Birth of Tragedy*, Nietzsche proposes that mythic forms hold two states of movement in tension: the Apollonian which offers rhythmic exactitude will be countered by the 'Dionysian rapture of the mass', most dramatically figured in the frenzy and chaos of Bacchic celebrations outside the city walls. This polarization of moral forces shapes aesthetic experience and has been a powerful contributor to movement philosophy. Rather than focus on formal properties of theatre that would be constrained by language and representation, Nietzsche suggests a 'play with intoxication' that can provide access to the expression of force such as is possible through dancing, in the body, and through ritual. And there is nothing stable about what he proposes:

The impelling *nous* starts suddenly, with frightful force – so fast, that in any event, that we must call its motion a 'whirl' … such a whirl must be infinitely strong not to be stopped by the load of the entire infinite world that is resting on it, [and] it must be infinitely rapid… The wider the concentric rings grow, the slower the movement may become. When the motion shall have reached the end of the infinite world,

at long last, it must need have attained an infinitely low
speed of revolution.

(Nietzsche 1996: 111)

This expanding whirl of movement produces a kind of delirium
that becomes a way to encounter another form of truth: a
transfiguration through an expanded and violent experience.
The high priest of a Nietzschean approach to movement in
theatre was director and writer Antonin Artaud, who in his
1938 book, *The Theatre and Its Double*, called for a theatre of
images, of plague and of cruelty. Such a cosmological theatre
– cosmological because dealing with the power of gods, fate
and eternal human struggles – requires a different kind of stage
language that cannot be dominated by the power of the text:

> For it must be understood, we intend to introduce silence
> and rhythm into the great number of moves and images
> arranged within a given time as well as a certain physical
> pulsation and excitement, composed of really created, really
> used objects and gestures. One could say the spirit of the
> most ancient hieroglyphics will govern the creation of this
> pure stage language.
>
> (Artaud 1970: 83)

For Artaud, the gestural dancing of the Balinese theatre
embodies this 'pure stage language', which 'seems like an
exorcism to make our devils flow' (Artaud 1970: 42). These
'metaphysicians of natural chaos dance' turn the experience
of theatre inside out, making its motivations expulsive and
ecstatic. Impassioned by theatre's capacity to make myth,
Artaud wanted theatre to begin with the senses – auratic and
visual – and secondly to transmit affect – both intoxicating and
rapturous (1970: 46). The formlessness of Artaud's ideas in
relation to the unbounded energies of the body, the instinctual
and irrational elements of the human psyche, and his move
towards an abstract theatre of images was almost impossible to
realize in art, particularly as Europe headed into the gruesome
realism of the Second World War. His contribution to theatre

theory is therefore that of divine seer, or poet–prophet, rather than theatre–creator.

For the post-war theatre directors Peter Brook and Jerzy Grotowski however, the opening of the body to extreme forms of performance practice represented opportunities to extend the 'cruelty' of Dionysius to a rigorous corporeal investigation of theatrical form. In theory then, the endurance of acting becomes understood as a form of esoteric devotion, where that pertains to the pursuit of the mystical in movement aesthetics. In *Towards a Poor Theatre* (1968), Grotowski expands upon the relationship between physical rigour in excess of pain and gestural expression. His ethos has several mantras: the 'holy actor', the 'via negativa' and the 'new testament'. With these religious overtones, he places the actor at the heart of theatrical experience, and it is their willingness to 'sacrifice' themselves to revelation in performance that is essential for the audience; hence the language of spirituality suggests a transcendence of the everyday through theatre. Beginning with the 'via negativa', the actor prepares by letting go of habits and 'trained' gestures in order to expose the psychic layers that determine hidden fears and joys. From first-hand experience of one of his workshops, his performers, such as Ludwig Flaszen and Zygmunt Molik, were hyper-athletes who trained intensively, often without rest breaks, over long periods, so that muscle strain and sweat were part of the bodily sensitizing. With strict adherence to these training principles for the actors, during the period in which Grotowski was still directing (until the late 1970s), the exercises were a means to an end, a disciplining that continued the work of Meyerhold and Stanislavski on movement plasticity for examining truth.

Exposed to the Russian theatre, however Grotowski refutes their methods – 'not just one mechanical (and therefore rigid) gesture of arm or leg, nor any grimace, helped by a logical inflection and a thought' because he seeks a different purpose for theatre: '(i)n the final result we are speaking about the impossibility of separating spiritual and physical. The actor should not use his organism to illustrate a "movement of the soul"; he should accomplish this movement with his organism'

(Grotowski 1968: 91). The 'holy actor' undertook their preparation with yoga training, from headstands to breathing techniques, but the extreme physical endurance could also push the actors to an exhaustion where a particular mental boundary was crossed; the 'peeling of onion layers'. This felt sense of the body 'in extremis' is well known to circus artists as much as to long-distance runners and can be both a source of pain as well as profound satisfaction from peak performance. At the moment of seeming physical inertia, in fact, a different intensification of experience may emerge as something more 'authentic' or revelatory. Extending the plasticity of the body as a 'resonator' for breath and voice, the leading Grotowski actor Ryzsard Cieslak could sculpt his 'organism' through isolation of different body parts – for instance, slipping flexibly from the centre of the spine, rippling through to arms, releasing the head and allowing a fish or bird to emerge and 'take off in flight' (1968: 105). Grotowski watched and waited for these instances of transfiguration, and only when a movement emerged were words spoken.

The theatre exercises for actors devised by Grotowski and his company remain a significant legacy although it is, however, a mistake to forget the swell of movement in his theatre productions. Nonetheless, Grotowski did not seek spontaneity in performance; instead the rehearsal process provided the score for an exacting theatre of 'authenticity' (1968: 192). The term 'authenticity' in contemporary theatre is a confusing one, but for Grotowski it relates to the moment-by-moment visibilizing of corporeal sensations in the service of acting; it was not a 'true' core, or something belonging to a particular identity, but rather a process of revelation tested in performance. Whether this 'authenticity' can ever be fully realized was not I believe important to Grotowski, but the dedication to exposing the idealizations and neglects of the social body was what he sought from the movement of actors. Perhaps this quest is best understood through continuing the case study of *The Constant Prince* that contrasts the approaches to theatre of Meyerhold's biomechanics with the ecstatic revelations of Grotowski.

Case Study #3, part b: *The Constant Prince* (1965)

The production by Grotowski of Calderón's *The Constant Prince* at his small Theatre of 13 Rows in Opole, Poland, in 1965 differs greatly from Meyerhold's grand Moscow stage, but they share a political lineage: this classic political morality play enables both directors to explore questions of authority and leadership under autocratic ideological rule. In Grotowski's production, the stage is stripped still further of historical or literal references to Calderón's play although the imagery relies heavily on the symbols of Catholic religiosity, and the plot is underpinned by the failure of the Catholic church to account for the sacrifice of human souls and bodies during the Holocaust (in which the concentration camps of Poland had been complicit only twenty years earlier).

The Grotowski theatre scholar Paul Allain (2017) calls Grotowski's theatre 'a gift to the audience', and in the stage-auditorium configuration, often an intimate relationship, the spectator is invited to participate in a ritual. In black-and-white photo documentation of Grotowski's Laboratory Theatre production, the audience peers down upon the performance space as if from an operating theatre or chapel balcony. While emphasizing the actor's spiritual apotheosis, Flaszen – in this production also a co-writer – writes of the play as 'a living hymn in homage to human existence' (Grotowksi 1968: 82). As I've explained, Grotowski seeks to explore the mutability of compassion in the performer and was not interested in the 'tragic pose' of the Prince beholden to his devoted followers. Instead, the chorus of actors resemble moving sculptures, at times perpetrators of persecution, at others silent witnesses, and if their faces shudder and smile, their eyes burn with intelligence. While they stalk and observe the immemorial violence done to Prince Ferdinand, Cieslak in the title role undergoes a kind of ecstatic metamorphosis.

A detailed reconstruction of the original work was created in Italy in 1977 and recorded on film. On a white-sheeted low bed, or wooden altar, a semi-naked man rests, arms extended, his bare torso heaving. Dressed in black seventeenth-century-style jackets and breeches, the other actors swirl around him alternately desperate to tease or attack him or to pray with him. When standing, Cieslak appears bowlegged with shirt open, and his head falls sideways as he chants a prayer. With his sensitized corporeal plasticity, as if a figure in a trance, the actor moves convulsively, stretching and bending like a starfish, but within moments he is crouched and bent double into a compact ball. With eyes closed, however, this actor exists in a different reality, his loincloth exaggerating the extent of his vulnerability and making him resemble a religious martyr. The Prince's religious experience endures as an ecstatic performance through a series of prolonged gestures – with energetic impulses of the inner organism switching rapidly from an abased pose, along an exposed neck with his head pressed back, to the licking of his tongue on the floor. When grabbed by the black figures and raced around the room, Cieslak's sparse frame shows his ribs rising and falling through the skin of his torso. Then, as he lies back in a sweat on the sheets, his eyes roll listlessly and one wonders if he will ever return from this embodied manifestation of martyrdom in the theatre.

This energetic approach to movement in theatre may seem far from the more pragmatic theories of Stanislavski and Meyerhold, but it does connect to theories of emotional memory and the notion that the body holds the history of its lived experience as a resource. Allain recounts (2017), for instance, that the role of the Constant Prince was constructed with Cieslak through his memories of being in love with a young girl in a repressive Catholic society. Very much a scholar of the theatre, Grotowski wanted dramaturgical structures to 'actualise their potentiality'; hence actors such as Cieslak needed to draw upon the theatre's psychophysical poetics. What Grotowski rejected were the tricks, masks and artifices of theatre forms that separated audience from actors, and actors from the submerged corporeal knowledge of an inner emotional sensibility.

If this is a theory, then it seems closer to a theory of ritual than to theatre, drawing as it does upon trance, and upon the body knowledge of movement somatics, to illuminate the psyche. The famous British theatre director Peter Brook, himself an artist on a quest, reflects upon Grotowski's theatre as a search for 'the great mystery of forms', in which the theatre laboratory tries to perceive 'the impulse of a totally unknown gesture':

> He wanted to attain pure impulse. An impulse is not visible, it has to be 'carried' by something and this carrier, this vehicle, is the human body. Through an intonation, through movements and gestures, he wanted to find, in a more and more precise and detailed manner, the relation between the internal energies of the body and their external expression.
>
> (Brook 2009: 67)

At stake in this approach to theatre seems to be a notion of the electrical or nervous system, as a current that stimulates the movement of the actor, a kind of over-charging that can release impulses that may have novel effects. Grotowski was not alone in these endeavours – obsessive, modernist and esoteric – to create a theatre of transfiguration, through practices that test the limits of the actor as a psycho-somatic organism. What is certain is that these corporeal movement practices have also borrowed extensively from non-Western training systems and philosophies such as yoga, while at the same time artists in Japan and South Asia were making their own experiments with how movement images become activated in the flesh of actors.

Assemblage: Butoh

The post-war Japanese genre of Butoh evolved during the 1960s but has extended into contemporary theatre with a wide range of esoteric movement practices and forms. The early creators of the genre, most notably Hijikata Tatsumi (1928–86) and Kazuo Ohno (1906–2010), were repelled by the idealization of bodies in traditional theatre and instead drew insight from the atypical movement of 'lepers, pariahs, prostitutes' (Baird 2012: 180). They began to experiment with movement exercises that could deconstruct and redistribute the manifestations of bodily energy in performance. Hijikata, for instance, wrote that 'only when, despite having a normal, healthy body, you come to wish that you were disabled, or had been born disabled, do you take your first step in butoh' (Baird 2012: 160). Such a complex relationship to movement was not about pretending to have, or imitating, a disabled body, which would be an offensive thing to do, but instead invites all performers to remember the experience of being unable to do something or feeling a part of the body disconnected or incomplete. The training system and philosophy of Butoh therefore require a transformation of perspective that is far from, indeed opposed to, the efficiency of production. A Butoh actor is not trying to execute the normalization of everyday gestures, nor are they aiming to improve the instrument of the body in order to be fit for purpose. Instead, the process of embodiment becomes 'assigned to imagine various things – such as being eaten by differing numbers of insects, or shocked by differing charges of electricity – with the assumption that the use of such imagery will qualitatively transform the movement (sometimes in extremely minute ways)' (Baird 2012: 7). Such contradictory qualities simultaneously require intense control; they must practise having 'eyes' all over the body (fingertips, back and feet) and develop ways to 'depict physically and mentally unfree marginalized characters' (Baird 2012: 175). A Butoh practitioner, like the Grotowski actors, will be trained to examine this inner process of sensory observation on a journey towards inner transformation.

Philosophically, then, it is not the freedom of the actor but the ways in which restrictions play out in the performance that are of most interest, hence the slowness and distorted bodily movements that often characterize Butoh. The teacher-artist Ohno explains how this esoteric movement quality is attained; the performance does not 'consist of a series of consecutive actions in time; they simply don't follow one another in linear sequence. Instead, one has the impression that he thrusts deeper and deeper into each and every movement and step, as though he were moving within each movement' (Ohno and Ohno 2004: 11). In my experience of watching Butoh performance, the muscles of the smallest action, such as a twitch in an elbow or the rising of the ribs, start to become visible. Very often shadowy forms that resemble ghostly but not quite-human figures fall into and across the stage. The mise en scène might be thought of as action-painting in slow motion, revealing inkblots that spread and blur across a canvas, sometimes adding clarity and at other times allowing the absurd or darkest forces of an image to emerge.

The theatre imagery of Butoh, as Japanese scholar Bruce Baird explains, derives from a surrealist aesthetic, juxtaposing Western and Eastern narrative fragments from literature, art, propaganda and the information age. Such imagery has, particularly with the earlier practitioners, been harnessed to political and social contradictions that arose from the horrors of war or the abandonment of humans to the machinery of capitalist progress. One famous exercise that is linked to the effects of the bomb in Hiroshima on the Japanese psyche is the 'Ash Pillar Walk' which imagines 'a human sacrifice that has been burned so completely that the only thing left is ash ready to crumble at any moment – it is all form with no faculties' (Baird 2012: 178). While many Western theorists have studied this form of theatre, linking it to both modern dance and the atomic bomb, Baird explains that the movement theories of Butoh are also embedded in a version of Taoist animism, in which information and elemental nature simultaneously hold and distribute power. The moving body becomes thus a conduit for an intensification of nerves, muscles and bones that are responsive and reactive to the surface qualities of earth, air and other tactile or imaginary stimulations that may also be embodied biographical memories. The task of the Butoh performer is to activate the micro-perceptions within the movement assemblage that will generate multiple, perhaps disorienting, associations for the audience. In these terms, the concept of movement as continuous flow, as smooth connections between one point and another, one articulation and another, can no longer be sustained. We might see instead a series of jerky interruptions to a gesture, or perhaps a trembling in the middle of a pathway towards a door, or a frenetic jumping on the spot; theatrically, such fragmented movements can have historical significance since they might embody responses to traumatic circumstances. In a performance of mixed ability actors for a Butoh Festival called 'Forbidden Laughter' in 2019, they also released the joy of forgotten or buried aspects of movement's theatrical potential.

Another contemporary take on Butoh has emerged with the artist Takao Kawaguchi reversing the immersive philosophical and practical regimes for acquiring this movement knowledge in his performance of *About Kazuo Ohno* (2016). Instead of romanticizing the rejection of modernity by moving reverently into communion with nature, Kawaguchi regards Butoh as a form of dance repertoire. Lacking the years of diligent Butoh training with inner impulses, Kawaguchi meticulously copied a series of emblematic performances from Ohno's extensive film and photographic archive for this production.

For example, *Admiring La Argentina* (1977) was Ohno's passionate tribute to a great flamenco dancer – and with great poetry and mystery, he channelled her bare wriggling arms, flinging feet and eloquent expressionist face. As Ohno aged and withered, he continued with faltering steps, and increasingly with broken hands and faded costumes, to trace her dance with his loving but imperfect body memory. Kawaguchi, on the other hand, ensures that the seams of this mimetic repertoire are fully visible. Downstage right, the costumes hang on a rack from which he takes off or puts on the paraphernalia that ghosts the cinematic images – feather boas, the dinner suit, tight-fitting bodices, white nylon stockings, paste-like make-up and silk cloaks. Manipulating the material remains, almost like playing in a junk shop with throwaway garments, Kawaguchi reproduces also the gesticulations and grimaces – fluttering hands, sideways tilt of the head, dissembling of the eyelids – that formed part of the affectivity of Ohno's performance but without the impassioned inner landscape.

As an audience, we are conscious of seeing a copy of an appropriated archive that has become an artefact of radical Japanese cultural expression. And yet, in spite of the distance between these different historical gestures, we have time to wonder: why is he flapping his arms like a bird? Or, appearing to weep hysterically? And now spinning like a whirling dervish? Just as the inspiration of Butoh intended with its attention to bodily fragmentation and inner assemblages, these re-inhabited movement images do manifest an alien corporeality, startling the spectator with the discomforting echo of Ohno as an auratic presence. It seems possible, for a moment, that the assemblage of such esoteric movement sutures memory to history: the remembrance of an enduring fantasy of cultural and gendered transmutation. Since Butoh aimed to quietly counter the overload of an information-based society, which had been instrumentalizing movement as effort in Western Europe, then these Japanese gestures are of a different, much quieter, less coherent order. Within the study of movement in the theatre, the recognition of the historical and social impacts of their dislocation and fragmentation seems to give performers, such as La Argentina, Ohno and Kawaguchi, access to an affective realism that remains impressively out of step with modernity.

Crowds: Canetti

In keeping with this book's counterpoint about movement as both individual and collective, the final part of this section will examine concepts of movement for theatre that derive from cultural sociology. From the perspective of theatre studies, the challenging argument of sociology is not that we are foremost social animals, nor that theatre needs better reflection of social attitudes to counter stereotypes performed both on and off the stage, although both are important. Rather, social theory positions the very idea of a 'system' under scrutiny, asking questions about whether social organizations can produce rational and progressive outcomes and whether theatre is like a system or indeed something else. It certainly makes sense to attend to the notion that an individual, as a system or centre of self-knowledge or sensory perception, does not exist in isolation. Bodies and selves are not monads, as Grotowski seems to suggest, with inner cores that can be stripped back, or realized, as the potentially liberated self. The corporeality of subjects is always, as feminist theorist Elizabeth Grosz argues, as much shaped by external efforts and forces as it is by inner propulsions or psychic imagination (1994: 12). Cultural theorists Norbert Elias, Michel de Certeau and Tim Ingold also regard the monadic individual as part of figurations that interweave with other figurations, creating interdependencies, and multiple forms of embodiment in any social system.

If the chorus was the collective formation of communal and ritualized forms of ancient theatre, aestheticized in the early twentieth century as a choral effect, I want here to consider the crowd, with all its resistant lumpen-ness, as a movement figuration of the twentieth century. Having emerged as bourgeois individuals in dramatic naturalism through the close-up of the face, the experience of individuation was dramatically challenged by its cinematic opposite, the anonymous mass who represent the formation and ideology of the crowd. The question of how crowds behave, and whether the collective force of crowds will subsume the individual, becomes then critical to thinking about group movement and theatrical representation.

Having witnessed the effect of fascism in coercing crowds and been disturbed by the 'society of the spectacle', Elias Canetti's book on *Crowds and Power* (1981) diagnoses the multiple types, symptoms and diseases of an assembled public. Traversing its long and tragic history from the animal to the human, the juridical to the political, the religious to the colonial, he writes that we inhabit crowds, and behave like crowds, even when we think we are most individual. Groups of people standing, lying down and sitting, for instance, will adopt a certain attitude when placed alongside those who cannot stand, lie or sit, and these preconditioned attitudes will arouse powerful feelings – laziness, pity, heaviness, fear (Canetti 1981: 453–5). Despotic rulers exploit the power of the crowd when they stand and command them: '[T]he stiller he stands, the less often he turns and looks about him, the more impressive he is' (Canetti 1981: 450); thus a leader can assert a brutal or intoxicating power. Such a coercion of movement is evident at political rallies as well as in military training and schools.

A dynamic component of the theatre apparatus is always the choreography of collective movement, for which Canetti makes a suggestion: '[T]he crowd needs a direction. It is in movement and it moves towards a goal. The direction, which is common to all its members, strengthens the feeling of equality' (1981: 32). While a coherent crowd can create the 'feeling' of belonging, such an invigorating and unifying force can also be terrifying. If one thinks of a football crowd in the stands, one can watch it swell, and the heads flow, as the players move with and towards the action of the ball. These effects are palpable and exciting – and yet when a fire breaks out or a stampede happens, the 'flight crowd' becomes dangerous. Perhaps for good reason, one of Artaud's metaphors for his theatre of cruelty was this irrational, multi-directional and infectious dynamic of panic or fear. When required to escape from something powerful and external, such as when a flood of people leave behind a war zone, and even if the emotional journey is overwhelming, the mass of bodily energies will become focused and coherent.

In terms of artistic representation such as in paintings and film, scenes of crowds provide markers of historical mood, social events and public reception. Crowds can connote the realism of street life, schools or festivals, but they also build dramatic effect, as with the 'density and equality' of sailors in Sergei Eisenstein's film *Battleship Potemkin* or soldiers storming a castle in the film *Lord of the Rings*: 'Everything here depends upon movement ... Density is embodied in the formal recurrence of retreat and approach; equality is manifest in the movements themselves. And thus, by the skilful enactment of density and equality, a crowd feeling is engendered' (Canetti 1981: 33). The appearance of a crowd, such as a lynch mob, also allows the drama of individual lives to seem more poignant, with one special narrative deserving attention, while all the other actors belong to the crowd who represent the ordinariness of the multitude. News reports are often constructed this way when they interview a sample individual to narrate their view of some major crisis.

Although modern drama's focus on the individual and the dramas of domestic life may seem disconnected from the crowd – its mentality and energetic forces – it has not been absent from the twentieth-century stage. The Austrian theatre director Max Reinhardt, for instance, tried to bring the theatrical crowd to fulfilment utilizing the techniques of symbolist aesthetics with cinematic lighting and expressive dancers to create the 'total art-work' (Styan 1982: 12). Following the ideas of Craig (referenced at the beginning of this section) and playwright August Strindberg, his actors became more like symbols of 'ideas, emotions and Fate' so, for instance, 'the hero [is] removed from reality whether he stands alone under the beams of the spotlight or amid the crowds surging around him. He is lost in the cosmos as the expression of the finite longings of an ecstatic poet, the leader of a crowd in the intoxication of revolution or simply a member of a choric ensemble' (Richard Samuel quoted in Styan 1982: 44).

One of the first directors to build large, lavishly decorated ensemble productions, Reinhardt also tightly choreographed crowd scenes that included the audience. For a 1911 production of Aesychlus's *Oresteia* in London, he recruited local drama students and boy scouts, and the rehearsals were orchestrated like a symphonic score – 'huddling diminuendi ... slowly paralyzing horror, the breathlessly expectant accelerandi, the catatonic rests ... and muted fade-outs' (Styan 1982: 125). Impressed by the thronging multitude, both in acclaim and in disdain, one of the London critics describes the effect: 'Moans and cries and shouts set the air throbbing, and crowd upon crowd of people surges in, and there the light breaks upon them, and they fall down suppliant and stretch out their hands, a whole nation of them, to one man – white-robed, bronze-breastplated – standing high above them, calm and stately, god-like' (Styan 1982: 81). In such spectacles, the terrifying aspect of the crowd that worries Canetti with its dual nature of misdirected energy and collective compliance becomes activated, leaving the audience in thrall to its massed power.

Perhaps when the crowd became recognized as an instrument of power in the mid-twentieth century – as the mass formation that could be manipulated by the commands of the leader – then the theatre and its audience also changed. According to Canetti, the command to be within a crowd is a request to become 'something alien', in a way that is 'different from all other actions', and unless for a musical theatre production or dance ensemble, rarely today does an ensemble of actors perform prolonged movements in unison (1981: 353). Contemporary theatre directors are more likely to magnify the dystopian aspects of crowd behaviour and emotion, although the staging of crowd scenes has returned in various ways through the focus on participation in immersive theatre as the final case study for this section shows.

Case Study #5: *Audience* (2011)

For Canetti, the theatre audience has ceased to be a chorus; at most we resemble a 'throbbing crowd', with tones muted to the murmur of quiet laughter and applause during and after the show (1981: 35). When the Belgian theatre company Ontroerend Goed created a work called *Audience* in 2011, they rigorously tested the proposition of audience 'stagnation', resembling in this sense earlier plays such as Peter Handke's *Offending the Audience* (1966). Ontroerend Goed's interrogation of the audience begins with apparently benign observations: an actor, who could be just an usher, instructs them on what behaviour is expected – turning off mobile phones, going to the toilet in advance, not eating or drinking, laughing yes, but 'if you want to cough, you should go outside, although that might signal that you dislike the work'.[1] Most importantly, the spectators of *Audience* are encouraged to clap to indicate appreciation of the show, whether they 'liked' it or not. As Canetti explains:

> Ideally actors play to full houses; the desired number of spectators is fixed from the start. People arrive on their own ... There they all sit, like a well-drilled herd, still and infinitely patient ... The strength of the applause is the only clue to the extent to which they have become a crowd; it is the only measure of this, and is valued accordingly by the actors.
>
> (1981: 41)

After the anonymous actor delivers the framing introduction on audience conduct, the seated audience sees filmed footage of themselves projected on a large screen that fills the stage. As it pans around the rows of seats, a voice-over from the camera operator describes the bodily and facial expressions of individuals who respond viscerally to the feeling of exposure. Extremes of delight and confusion are magnified – turned-down mouth, wrinkled-up eyes, the fall of the hair – and observed much like the facial mobility of Henry Irving at the beginning of this section. Giving an imaginary voice to their inner thoughts of discomfort, the camera person also comments inappropriately on their dress and proffers audience statistics – 'you are all white' or 'six of you are homosexual'. An uneasy compliance and amusement marks this part of the show, particularly when the actors wheel in a clothes rack with coats and bags that were cloaked by the audience and start to try them on as a fashion parade. The 'crowd' plot becomes ever more cruel when a member of the audience is singled out because she refuses to join in with a clapping sequence that leads up to a standing ovation. With the camera zoomed in, the actor offers brutal insults: 'you look beautiful but fuck-face, is that the best you can do to make people feel sorry for you'. The audience is increasingly uncomfortable and he offers to stop if asked. As he explains 'this is a conceptual play ... ', but then he continues, 'I'm not going to stop until you spread your legs' and counts down on his fingers. With this degrading banter presented as the knowing complicity of theatre, the audience 'as crowd' is thus required to disaggregate and to act as individuals in response to this harassment.

Later scenes show historic footage of diverse crowds in military uniforms, at gospel churches, and dissidents being water-cannoned, and what is unmistakeable is the extent to which individual movement can become submerged by the mass. Canetti argues that there will always be a difference between 'the silent people and those who joined in' and that we cannot be sure how either will be judged. Such is the evidence in the aftermath of war or disaster. Affectively in this performance – the girl's knees shaking, for instance – the expectation of audience participation, whether active or passive, commands that we relinquish belief in autonomous movement to the power of crowd movement. Whether disdainful or fascinated, members of the audience respond to this challenge in different ways so that in the aftermath critical assessment is divided.

In contemporary immersive and participatory theatre, the choreographing of movement extends from sitting in the auditorium of a proscenium arch theatre to situations and spaces where audience mobility and interaction are essential to the performance. Site-specific works, such as Punchdrunk's *Sleep No More* (2011), and many smaller, even intimate, pieces ask the audience to make choices about how to stand, sit, listen, walk, touch and generally move with the mise en scène or the environment. Even with increasing agency given to the spectator, implicit claims about crowd passivity or group coercion are, as with Oentroerend Goed's production, often structured into these works since they rely on a degree of risk or trust for their fulfilment. With crowd movement, whether on or off the stage, as part of the contemporary theatre experience, as this final example suggests, Canetti's analysis of group or mass movement offers some valuable insights.

Conclusion

This section has detailed how the establishment of systems for using and interpreting theatre movement has contributed to theories of the actor. In particular, I have aimed to show that twentieth-century theatre has been strongly influenced by leading practitioners and theorists who have developed distinctive movement training and ideologies. As we have progressed through diverse compositional and instructional approaches, several key movement concepts have been examined, those of plasticity, effort, dynamics and intensity. With close analysis of these corporeal concepts in movement systems, this section has considered performances that traverse the phenomenology of naturalism, with its micro-impressions of gendered violence, and the nuances of historical memory in Butoh, through to the expansive energies of the crowd. The resounding argument is that theatre dramaturgy has many ways to structure, systematize and formalize the relationship between movement and embodied action, and therefore close examination of sample productions shows how actors' movement has been theorized and practised. Theatre is thus a vital resource to appreciate the experimental diversity and potential of movement as method and communication.

SECTION THREE

Movement in Contemporary Theatre

In the Introduction, we looked at three influential philosophical concepts for the understanding of movement in theatre: the vitality of being, the very attribute of life force in things; the role of learned and cultural techniques in shaping the body and its movement repertoire; and the role that rhythm plays in establishing patterns of difference in social life. In Section One, we examined the different ways in which historical changes have orchestrated understandings of movement in theatrical representation. These different theories include ideas about choruses and processions, gesture and stylisation, organic poetics and automata, plot and spectacle, and audiences that arise in specific periods of significant innovation, often because modes of performance instantiate logics in wider circulation within a given society or culture. The formal innovations are also stored, latent and residual, in the archive of theatre's history, hence available for reinvention by contemporary artists. In Section Two, these considerations of theatrical form are extended by the drive towards systematization and efficiency of corporeal movement in the modern drama and theatre of the twentieth century. Powerful ideas about the corporeal plasticity of the actor, the role that dynamics play in orchestrating stage action, and the esoteric impulses and crowd energies that lead towards cathartic or ritualized experiences have been investigated by modern theatre's many practices. Theatre, with this dynamic interplay between action and concept, has therefore generated theories of movement as much as it has illustrated or adopted theories from literature, film, philosophy, biology or social science. It is, one might say, a movement-machine, an apparatus for thinking about how and why movement matters.

To step now into the contemporary is to consider what differences apply to our present time. How do ideas about theatre differ from previously? Is there a way to think of movement as always and forever a measure of vitality, technique and rhythm, even when it falls out of step or moves against the grain? Are there conditions that change how we perceive movement and if so what are they? And how might we make theatre that responds, in movement, to the concerns of our times? In Section Three, I propose four frames to assist our thinking about these questions of movement in contemporary theatre: velocity (speed and slowness), animation and force. First, we consider movement along the dimensions of time, effectively fast and slow, and then on the dimension of the trajectory, that of animation and force. Speed is important because velocity communicates what amount of force is required to move the mass of a given object or event along a trajectory; it is also a political condition. We experience acceleration as a condition of theatrical movement, what might be called 'pace' as we discussed in relation to Roman comedy in Section One but it is also an element of 'dynamics' from Section Two. I have divided this dimension into two parts because the implications of speed and slowness, whether in racing, cooking, meeting schedules or theatre, are considerable. Animation, on the other hand, is a frame that returns to the question of how the 'anima' moves, asking what are the energetic realities (of bodies, characters, actions and stories) that animate a work of theatre? And the concept of force reminds us that there are externalities to movement, ways in which movement is sanctioned and commanded by ideologies that shape bodies and relations with time, space and effort. Consideration of these four framing concepts informs the stand-alone case studies, which will be followed by a brief conclusion.

There have been however seismic shifts in terms of what constitutes theatre in the twenty-first century, and so underpinning my analysis of these four frames of movement are the dramaturgical and aesthetic understandings of postdramatic theatre and intermedial performance with which contemporary artists make work. Significantly, the European theatre theorist Hans-Thiess Lehmann in his book *Postdramatic Theatre* (2006) argued that theatre is no longer tied to the legitimacy and representational logic of the dramatic text because it incorporates a range of semi-autonomous scenic crafts such as sound composition, lighting design, the movement score and spatial architecture. Key components of the burgeoning world of postdramatic theatre are 'gestures and movement', and he provides numerous examples of contemporary directors (Robert Wilson, Jan Fabre, Tadeusz Kantor, Jan Lauwers) who score and manage stage space with choreographic precision, working with bodies as if automatons, or who produce choric events complete with incantation and oblations (2006: 25). Where this shift towards a movement-based theatre has had most profound effect is on the relationship with spectators:

Text, body and space produce a musical, architectonic and dramaturgical constellation that results from predefined as well as 'unplannable' moments: everyone present senses their presence, sounds, noises, position in space, the resonance of steps and of words. It induces them to be careful, circumspect and considerate with respect to the whole of the situation, paying attention to silence, rhythm and movement. As theatre is thus understood as a 'situation' it simultaneously takes a step towards the dissolution of theatre *and* to its amplification.

(Lehmann 2006: 124)

More specifically, for him, movement forms part of a visual dramaturgy that emphasizes repetition and duration, and from this situation the viewer relates 'physically to sequences of movements in order to know the temporal movement in the image' (2006: 157). That means that movement is, among other things, a synesthetic relation we have to the sensory kinaesthesia of a person, object or image. Take, for example, a figure who stands shivering on stage, while in the background a large fan is blowing draped curtains; we easily put together the two images; the breeze is causing the curtains to move and the figure to shiver. If, however, we remove the fan and the figure shivers more and more violently in front of stationary curtains, we have a somewhat different response. We may wonder what is causing the figure to shiver, but imagine that it is not a breeze but something terrifying instead, and we experience the image of the shivering body, particularly if it lasts for some time, through the sensory responses of our own bodies, perhaps recalling a range of similar sensations or memories of fear, coldness or stress. In this kind of postdramatic theatre, we may not have many clues as to why the person was shivering, but as Lehmann argues 'through their own sense of time, imagination, empathy and the capacity to relate physical to sequences of movements, the viewers come to know the temporal movement in the image' (2006: 157). It is these movement relations which stimulate our imagination and contribute to our aesthetic interpretation of the mise en scène.

In addition to this heightening of the visceral sensations of corporeal movement, other changes to the perception of temporal movement have come from the increasing mediatization of theatre as it incorporates new technologies that enhance and modify representation. Theorizing the experience of performance through the lens of 'intermediality' includes all manifestations of theatre mediated by digital and recording technologies, although the omnipresence of digital culture in everyday life – social media, smartphone cameras and videos, headsets etc. – has meant that there is often little separation between embodied and virtual movement.

Much as cultural critic Walter Benjamin argues took place in the modern reproduction of photographs for the visual image, recording technologies may threaten the distinctive and autonomous idea of theatre as the unique live presence of the actor (Benjamin 1992). Theatre scholar Mathew Causey suggests that 'the (dis)appearance of theatre' in virtual spaces using digital simulation can be seen in the negative because it 'seeks to infect information from within while colonizing the body through science and technology' (2006: 180). For others, however, theatre's tools of representation are subject to reproduction as much as other media; hence we now have increasingly hybrid recorded and live events, relaying images from screen to stage and back. The Imaginarium *Tempest* mounted by RSC and Intel that we discussed in Section One, with its silvery apparition of Ariel floating on the shoulders of Prospero, provides just one example of the extent to which digital technologies expand movement potential. Nicholas Salazar-Sutil extends his diagnosis of such virtual movement to digital data itself, which he describes as a genre of 'online kinesis': characterized 'by a loss of physical connection with a networked sense of global space, and with a condition of perpetual movement and ceaseless activity' (2015: 213).

For theatre scholar Andy Lavender, on the other hand, the playful experimentation of intermedial theatre might be thought of as pleasurable; because we experience 'movement of a different sort ... like a machine, with an ineffable fluency to the conjunction of sound, utterance, action and imagery' (2010: 34). According to Lavender, these aesthetic constructions and phenomenal effects that arise from intermedial performance do not exist in any simple binary relation between organic principles or their digital equivalences. Movement is thus neither purely embodied nor purely virtual, rather multiple states and configurations of data and electronic circuits facilitate the representations of movement caused by the creative and coercive forms of affective, cognitive and immersive simulation. Importantly, digital movement as we move closer to the era of AI will involve machines sensing like humans, and translating back to us, in the form of data, facets of experience that we incorporate into the ontology of human subjectivity, and thus what we consider theatre.

Before we look at these new theatre genres, the postdramatic and the intermedial, a third configuration of contemporary theatre must articulate the collective and spatial dimensions of another movement principle at this moment in time. In the writing of poststructural theorists Giles Deleuze and Felix Guattari, many movement metaphors are used to describe collective formations – molecularities, deterritorializations, becomings, flocks, war machines and nomadism. If we select just one, the concept of nomadism (that is, a kind of figure who roams or has no fixed place of address), then we may begin to think about the notion of subjects, persons or objects that are not contained by the structural hierarchies, in transport from idea to idea, that organize knowledge. Rather, a nomadic existence, outside domestic or urban norms, contrasts with rigid boundaries and definitions of place, politics and art, as Deleuze and Guattari explain:

> The nomad has a territory; he follows customary paths; he goes from one point to another; he is not ignorant of points (water points, dwelling points, assembly points, etc.). But the question is what in nomad life is a principle and what is only a consequence.
>
> (1987: 380)

This figure of the nomad proposes that an existence outside the structure of the home and family unit sanctioned by dominant political structures also has knowledge of their own pathways and forms of survival. A homeless person, to take an urban example, still knows where it is safe to sleep at night, where they can get food from a soup kitchen, and how to assist their fellow nomads. Is 'sleeping rough' a principle of choice, or a category of government intervention, or is it a consequence of a society that has not provided sufficient care of vulnerable individuals? While negative connotations are often attached to the nomad, there are also affirmative and potentially productive realizations about the immaterial world acquired within nomadic existence, such as appreciation of places of communal shelter and solidarity. With this theory, Deleuze and Guattari elaborate further on the importance of the journey: 'A path is always between two points, but the in-between has taken on all the consistency and enjoys both an autonomy and a direction of its own' (1987: 380).

What Deleuze and Guattari are suggesting is that the nomad journeys on pathways, like the structure of a plot in a play, inhabited or uninhabited, known or less well known, that develop a direction of their own. Nomads may be marginalized, nonetheless they will reside, hide and foster their 'autonomy', such as incipient ways of moving and giving voice to their mobility. This notion can be extended to radical ideas that might disappear for a while, such as the role of talking in theatre or even of gods appearing on stage, before the potential for new alignments and new forms of meaning can arise from such concepts. The nomad is thus perhaps like the jester, who signifies the potential for the unknown to arise from outside conventional models of representation. The productions that I will discuss in this section are therefore connected to these moments of journeying between places and finding out, to return to Aristotle's phrasing, what kind of potentiality arises from the actualities of the nomad in contemporary theatre.

Feminists such as Rosi Braidotti (1994) have taken up this concept of the nomadic subject to examine the deterritorialization of women, migrants and refugees, rendered stateless by war, conflict and terror – hence to theorize movements that are forced upon those most dispossessed of a fixed identity. Other postcolonial and feminist theorists have suggested that the nomad may raid the colonizer's cupboard, steal his language and tools, to rearrange or mock the authority of imperial, racial and gendered discourses and signs (Bhabha 1984; Butler 2006). The nomad is the figure who moves between desire lines, who rewrites the territorial map otherwise. Many artists are nomads of a sort, because they instruct their audiences in practices of critical, geopolitical nomadism – utilizing movement principles for imagining justice in the twenty-first century.

In theatre, this idea of the nomad is suggestive for the formation of movement as a practice that is not always predictable in modernist terms by way of technique, nor representational by way of subject or character, but rather, the nomadic acknowledges that strange, resistant and uncomfortable movements will come to inhabit the space of performance. Theatre movement understood as nomadic will include processes for finding corporeal languages that exist in the gaps not currently defined or enabled by dominant political structures or commodified modes of expression. The internet has enabled some forms of this nomadic reinvention of movement to thrive. Hybrid or intercultural dance styles, enhanced by geographic and technological mobility, include, for instance, mergers between movement genres such as rumba and martial arts, street dance and Bollywood. Hand gestures have been universalized as emoticons, and other forms of sign language and facial vocabulary have surfaced in Instagram exchanges. Other movement genres from villages and Indigenous communities have, however, become marginalized and lost through urbanization and global transmission. But just as exciting are new opportunities for theatrical expression being claimed through the movements of differently gendered, sexed, abled and racialized communities. Aesthetic signification becomes mobilized then, not merely by representation of familiar ways of moving, or in the most incredible craft, but through a sensory awareness of the confluence of kinaesthesia, displacement, weight and gravity at work on different bodies.

The implications of some of these ideas about movement in contemporary theatre, such as its semi-autonomy from the text, its imbrication in digital life and its resistance to known pathways or habituated uses of the body, will play out in the following case studies. And they do, I hope, extend our interest in the ways that movement is subject to both inner and outer forces that shape and make the experiential, and sensory, aspects of theatre become 'live' for us. In the sense that perceptions of movement are both internal and observational, and eminently social and political, at one and the same time, the modes of analysing movement continue to evolve.

With one production widely seen in the global festival circuit (with script available), a prominent performance artwork, and four productions that are more locally specific and dramaturgically diverse, the focus in this section is postdramatic and intermedial theatre in which the temporal and spatial, cultural and political, dimensions of momentum are under interrogation.

Speed: *Attempts on Her Life*
(1997, 2007)

In 1997 the British playwright Martin Crimp's radical new play *Attempts on Her Life* was first staged at the Royal Court Theatre, London, and in 2007 director Katie Mitchell remounted the show for the National Theatre (NT). This latter production forms the basis of the case study and I was fortunate enough to view a video in the National Theatre archives as well as read the production notebooks, programme notes and rehearsal schedules.[1] Mitchell chose not to accelerate the date of the production forward to the post-September 11 world but to leave it set in 1997, a world without Twitter but with an incipient digital reality of live television, mobile phones and computers. It also followed on from her highly successful intermedial production of Virginia Woolf's *The Waves* for the National Theatre in 2006, in which the actors manipulated recording devices, sound effects, screens and other projections while playing all the characters in full view of the audience. Likewise, this production of *Attempts on Her Life* was played in continuous motion with the actors simultaneously managing the technologies of representation.

Opening to a bare stage and pumped-up electronic music in Mitchell's production, eleven actors (men, women, racially diverse, different ages) all well dressed in black outfits are shouting at the audience from the front of the stage. They are all speaking rapidly with overlapping accounts of what is happening somewhere off-stage:

> The woman? / young and beautiful, naturally / The man? ... Doing what? / Making love ... A panorama of the entire city / ... This whole tragedy of ideology and love / ... And now she's angry ... She begins to shout ... She beats and beats / and beats.
>
> (Crimp 1997: 5–9)

Standing in a line, jostling one another, we see them throwing their arms around, a habitual gesture to add emphasis that seems rather ineffective – pointing hands, slapping hands, reaching out, rolling cuffs and holding something out in front. I recall someone saying 'tragedy unfolds everywhere' although the script says instead: 'It's a universal thing in which we recognise, we strangely recognise ourselves. Our own world. Our own pain' (16). A buzzer goes off, and everyone runs to the back of the open stage – with the lights coming up on a scene set in a TV studio, with a woman, relaxed and smoking a cigarette, pontificating about the status of Annie – offering deadpan humour as she rolls around on her studio chair.

This complex play, regarded as a 'post-everything' critique of commodity and celebrity culture, has no characters and the scenes are unnumbered. With no obvious stage directions, the seventeen rapid-fire, unrelated scenes can be performed in any order and with as many people as the company or director wishes. The play revolves around a woman named by multilingual variations of Anna, Anh or Annie who is described in detail, evoked and questioned, but never appears. Meanwhile, lines assigned to each performer discuss family, art, technology, Europe, friendship, time-travel, suicide and terrorism. This episodic structure piles up associations, according to Aleks Sierz, with the war in Yugoslavia, the AIDS crisis and the privatization of state assets; however, the play is also a remarkably coherent essay on speed (Sierz 2007).

Movement concepts occur in rapid succession – Scene 7: The New Anny; Scene 8: Particle Physics; and Scene 9: The Threat of International Terrorism – and if such a decentred text can have a climax, these scenes make time speed up, uncertainty quicken and the heart race.

Speed, according to the cultural theorist Paul Virilio, impacts on the experience of the body, not through excessive motion but through sedentariness, which might be called 'the instant of absolute speed'; we believe we are moving but in fact nothing is changing even though we virtually feel as if we have moved. We bank in Hong Kong, we make love in New York, and we weep over the collapse of Notre Dame in Paris, all within the space of a few minutes. Speed is also the by-product of new forms of technology, and of habitation, that are ironically 'without movement', which is a state of existence that Virilio calls 'dromology', a state of contemporary being that impacts on the individual capacity to participate in civic life. As Virilio explains in a 1999 interview, speed 'is not a phenomenon, but rather the relationship between phenomena. In other words, it is relativity itself. We can go further and say that speed is a milieu. It doesn't just involve the time between two points, but a milieu that is provoked by a vehicle' (cited in Redhead 2004: 44). The vehicle here is not just a car or an airplane but may also be social or news media in which instants of time happen very fast and yet are geographically distant. In digital culture, as Salazar-Sutil suggested earlier, this digital kinaesthesia also signals an end to bounded identity, thus precipitating further transformations of movement representation in theatre: who or what is moving? we might ask.

Mitchell is one of several contemporary directors whose approach to making theatre has included articulation of the polyvalent harmonies in Greek plays, the phenomenology of Woolf's novel and, more recently, the hidden atmospheric tensions of Shakespeare's character, Ophelia. With training in the Stanislavskian method and influenced by the choreographer Pina Bausch, many of Mitchell's productions utilize an expressive style of dance theatre but her more recent works have also been complex intermedial events in which onstage actors perform and manipulate the technologies of vision. So, to put Crimp's and Virilio's ideas in dialogue, how does Mitchell translate speed not as metaphor but as active force into the time-space of her production of *Attempts on Her Life*?

In Scene 7, Anny is a new model car, described in the exhilarated, hyperbolic terms of advertising, with 'telecommunications networks ... collapsing the close shots of time and space' as the new Anny supercharges its way around Europe. A Northern European woman in sleek black leather suit speaks in a solo spot in a foreign language – the 'new Anny' is hence translated or spoken twice, almost as if changing gears as it crosses borders. The scene is seductive although the narrative is increasingly vulgar and barbaric. Like all war machines, this vehicle has no place for human detritus – 'for the degenerate races ... for the mentally deficient ... or the physically imperfect' (Crimp 1997: 32–3) – and it emphatically lists acts of pillage, rape and torture that 'No one ... No man ... No one ... ' (34) would dare to commit in this car. In the face of the camera, the woman's face licks her lips, grotesquely opposing the violence of the imagery, mockingly horrible 'Melted chocolate. Yum, yum, yum' (34). This convergence between women, transport and violation – 'Financial packages subject to status' (35) – produces the vision of a pure capitalist purchase on reality. Mitchell follows the seduction with a pornographic burlesque dance, complete with strippers, and then a close-up film sequence of an older woman wearing a bib and being fed yogurt by spoon. These scenes are not in Crimp's script, but they follow the course of a woman's abjection, and as she bubbles through the white sticky goo on her face, the action is accompanied by background laughter. Needle insertions into a breast shown in triplicate – live and through a split screen – simultaneously replicate the precise action, the intensification of an affect, the propulsion or pace of the scene, and its disruption by external forces.

The production notes further reveal Mitchell's process of dramaturgical acceleration including complex technical plotting for hooks (for clothes), for cigarette and fire putting out, for lighting, for microphones and cameras, props and furniture, lighting effects, and flys. A 'list of competition rules [is] established for the actors', and there is extensive concern with camera moves as well as specific notes, such as 'Dina Korzun might require 2 identical pairs of shoes due to her having to put her feet in the sand'. While the actors actually move very little, multiple objects are in constant movement, with pages dedicated to detailing where false nails, handbags, rings and lanyards need to be placed, observing that 'due to the busy nature of our transitions and the fact we are using liquids on stage' that everyone must conform to health and safety requirements.

Given the rapid juxtaposition of critical events – terrorist incidents, war crimes, gallery openings, news reports – Virilio would argue that politics has become synonymous with this changed reality, since each new technology precipitates its own 'accidents' and thus its own crises: 'We are experiencing an epoch that spells the international, the global accident. This is the way I interpret simultaneity and its imposition upon us, that is, the omnipresence of the information bomb' (cited in Redhead 2004: 47). This violent temporality of the 'information bomb' has effects on bodily movement that invert the effects of speed by entrenching and establishing sedentariness as a kind of 'polar inertia'. We might appear to travel, as Anny does, but we may also go so fast that we don't see anything, don't experience anything, but rather just accumulate short bursts of gravitational pull experienced as 'immediacy, simultaneity, instantaneity and ubiquity' (Virilio 2010: 74). Likewise, the premise of *Attempts on Her Life* is that none of the scenes presented are necessarily true; they provide accounts, delocalized and instantaneous, of ubiquitous generality. Perhaps Annie/Anny/Anne/Ana/Anh is Chinese, or Indian, or American, but as theatregoers, we want to believe that a character is unique and still intelligible, although each so-named actor might be all of us, global travellers, or none, as subject of the drama. Mitchell's production ends with the actors lined up again at the front of the stage, trying to recount what has happened; there is quite a lot of laughter, seeking definitions of words, all in disagreement, then their voices accumulating as they group into clusters to understand the horror of Annie's disappearance. Since a postdramatic work does not need resolution, the actors are slowly sucked into a shaft under the stage. In disappearance, the movement seems to replicate the performance's opening and therefore flattens time into the continuous present.

Crimp's play appears to offer little hope for contemporary theatre because it participates seductively in the acceleration technologies that Virilio identifies in the 'pitiless' aesthetics of modern art – able to 'freeze all originality and all poetics in the inertia of immediacy' (2003: 47). Mitchell thrives in this milieu with pop choruses singing the 'Girl Next Door'; particle physics disintegrating on film; broken-up voices, distributed across even single sentences; and the swirling of the cameras. The play itself has become a giant particle accelerator because it has been a popular choice for school and university performance ensembles, with plenty of scope to invent the experience of 'speed' through recording technologies, phones and flash costumes. The 'portable revolution', as Virilio argues, involves thinking how to live with speed, how to maintain a grip on motility and our disembodied comportment in contemporary media channels of communication (2010: 78). With its violent allusions to imminent death, this theatre production of *Attempts on Our Life* helps us to understand how the coercive power of speed-as-inertia is being staged in contemporary political culture.

Slowness: *The Artist Is Present* (2010)

By way of contrast to speed, I want to consider what we might call 'slow theatre', a theatre in which pausing the flow of movement can sustain and shift the attention, or conscious and unconscious perceptions, of an audience. Perhaps we just watch an actor sitting on a bench or smoking a cigarette or find ourselves required to patiently wait for something to happen. For performers, wilful constraints upon physical exertion may be determined by the script, but they can emerge spontaneously when you freeze, forgetting your lines, and the darkness opens up before you, or when you hold the audience as if in a state of rapture. At such temporal injunctions, the lack of movement or an ill-defined immobility seems to rupture the border between actor and audience: it is as if performer and audience touch one another. Such an aesthetics of stillness may replace the necessity to 'act' or to produce action from representation on the mainstream stage, whereas in performance art, the experience of duration is designed to heighten awareness of presence. The following examples examine how the limits of slowness in modern drama represented the experience of being there in real time.

Twentieth-century dramatists such as Jean Genet, Luigi Pirandello, Eugène Ionesco, Samuel Beckett and Harold Pinter frequently regarded the human condition as absurd; believing to exist is also to produce human suffering. This nihilistic view of human agency, unable to realize transformation or social change, is portrayed in Western theatre, such as in Jean Paul Sartre's *No Exit* (1944), as entrapment or lack of movement. For Beckett, however, reducing dramatic action to stasis became a way to contemplate the inevitability of stillness, the cessation of mobility and a kind of death in life. Beckett's characters – such as Winnie in *Happy Days* stuck in sand up to her waist and then her neck or the woman in the chair in *Rockaby* (1980), 'time she stopped, going to and fro' – seem to be depicted as 'professional waiters, caught in the machinery of interrupted dynamics' (Bryden 2004: 180). Translating this Beckettian stasis into performance places unique demands upon actors, but once bodily movement is limited and the force of language is restricted, performance reaches a physical and metaphysical limit. I was privileged to watch a performance of Beckett's late novella, *Worstward Ho*, choreographed by Maguy Marin in Paris in 2008. With an intermittent and almost inaudible voice-over, almost no movement took place on a blackened stage for nearly forty minutes. A shudder from underneath a mound of black cloth produced a sensation on my eyelids that was all the difference between a glimmer of light and no light. Given that the text focuses on the exhaustion of the body, of place, of speech and of life itself, this 'meremost minimum' of presence left the audience sensing only the movement of their own breath and eyelids in the 'dimmest light as never' (Beckett 1984). When I left the theatre with a friend, we both burst out laughing with relief in the night outside, almost delirious with freedom from the pressure and pain of staring into the void.

Lehmann also notes the amplification that takes place in the slow motion of much contemporary postdramatic theatre: 'When physical movement is slowed down to such an extent that the time of its development itself seems to be enlarged as through a magnifying glass, the body itself is inevitably *exposed* in its concreteness. It is being zoomed in on as through the lens of an observer and is simultaneously "cut out" of the time–space continuum' (2006: 164). Thus, postdramatic theatre might use slowness to intensify discomfort, but with its focus on the quality of 'image-time', the elongated pause also fine-tunes our perceptions, asking the audience to listen to the thoughtfulness of a time and place.

Dance theorist Andre Lepecki takes this insight still further. He argues that discourses of twentieth-century dance have been dominated by the passion for energetic movement, and indeed claims about performance as an autonomous art independent of sculpture, poetry or music are often linked to the uniqueness of movement. The emphasis on flow and movement efficiency that we discussed in Section Two has been privileged by colonial and class politics so that signs of activity are preferred over passivity, and the expansive, controlling gesture is admired more than the refusal to move or be moved. We might also recall, however, Mauss, noting that 'rest is the absence of movement' in Section One and hence a necessary aspect of the philosophy and techniques of movement. As Lepecki writes, kinaesthetic epistemologies are ways of inhabiting the body that 'associate the force of movement with a politically positive dynamics' but this strand of modernist thought has been or is now 'exhausted' (Lepecki 2006: 13). Following the work of anthropologist Nadia Serermatakis, Lepecki suggests an alternative to the constancy of movement lies in the 'still-act' that may quietly rupture the 'flow of the present': 'Stillness is the moment when the buried, the discarded, and the forgotten escape to the social surface of awareness like life-supporting oxygen. It is the moment of exit from historical dust' (Lepecki 2006: 15). Instead of movement as activity, and the flow of dramatic narrative or physical virtuosity, practising stillness and allowing the past to be remembered in the body, in the event and exchange of performance contributes to an alternative aesthetic for theatre.

States of stillness and the slow time of movement are the intense focus of many durational performances such as those created by Marina Abramović over the course of her career, but most prominently with the 2010 work, *The Artist Is Present*, presented at the Museum of Modern Art in New York. This performance involved Abramović sitting in a chair in front of a table with another empty chair on the other side of the table and facing her. Anyone in the gallery could step forward and seat themselves opposite her and she would gaze directly into their eyes. With these deceptively simple instructions, Abramović spent 736 hours (nearly 3 months), 8 hours a day (and once a week, 10 hours) practising being present to another person. Over the course of the 736 hours more than 1,500 people sat with her, some of them for more than an hour while others chose to stay just a few minutes. There was no script, and no obvious preparation for the event, except that it became so popular that audience members had to wait in a queue for many hours to get an opportunity to sit in the chair.

For Abramović, on the other hand, the practice of immobility demanded extreme discipline, the kind of discipline that overcomes the bodily expectations of eating, urinating, itching, sneezing and otherwise feeling restless. In a sense, she had prepared for this performance for most of her adult life, not only in earlier durational works but during long periods living in the desert with Aboriginal Australians or in solitary meditations at Buddhist retreats. In many previous performances, her experimentation with enduring and surpassing pain as a practice of bodily liminality was a self-conscious fulfilment of torture and desire, accompanied by a degree of exhibitionism. Abramović was however also investigating how an altered consciousness of the material aspects of the world, in the form of rocks, man-made objects, clothing, money and architecture, enters into new alignments with the immaterial. For instance in a public shopping centre in Tokyo for a piece called *Black Dragon* (1994), Abramović placed rose quartz blocks at different heights on a wall for people to rest their heads on; she believed these stone pillows would open up different thought patterns for shoppers who stopped their daily routines. Another of the over-determining facets of material reality in Abramović's performance art is the experience of time, so an 'act' of performance will frame time as a long period of hours or days in which the artist passes a threshold of consciousness by surrendering to the experience of the moment. In *Night Crossing*, a durational work performed twenty-two times between 1981 and 1986 with her then-partner Ulay (artist Frank Uwe Laysiepen), they sat across from each other in front of a table making eye contact for eight hours a day. In the simplicity, and yet extreme difficulty, of this arrangement, the focus was on the practice of being present to the other person. In *The Artist Is Present*, this formidable task was instead assigned to her encounter with the audience.

For the performance at the Museum of Modern Art (MOMA), Abramović needed to be still throughout the day, and even though she experienced excruciating pain in her back and ribcage from the chair, she abided by her own rules of performance not to change the situation but endure it. Her task was to open her eyes to each new person who sat before her and for them to gaze at each other. What she found in the process was an extreme form of intimate exchange, a looking that allowed others to pause and open themselves up to their inner feelings, as Abramović explains in her memoir: 'What I found immediately was that the people sitting across from me became very moved. From the beginning, people were in tears – and so was I. Was I a mirror? It felt like more than that. I could see and feel people's pain' (2016: 309).

While Abramović moved very little, perhaps only blinking occasionally, with some onlookers thinking she was like a plaster statue, movement still happened – 'people sitting across from me became very moved' – whether they needed to wriggle in the chair or tears welled up or a half-smile appeared on their lips, there was something moving in the energy between them. The physical stillness and the slowed time created space for a complex repertoire of affective movements within each individual's corporeal and psychic memory to become alive. Abramović was herself surprised at the extent of pain that her voluntary audience brought to the performance even when, or perhaps because of, being witnessed by others in the gallery. Her intense concentration gave them permission to just sit, be received and allow emotions to surface and move between them. Abramović also writes of the moment in which she exchanged looks with her former lover and collaborator, Ulay, after many years of separation. When she opened her eyes to see who was the next person in the chair opposite, 'twelve years of my life ran through me in an instant' (2016: 313). From beyond the duration of their romantic and artistic partnership they gazed at each other, allowing unwitting tears of sorrow, anger and tenderness to appear from within that shared history until, breaking her own rules, Abramović reaches out and holds his two hands. The slow theatre of her durational performance over the entire period did not so much stop or still time, but the consciousness of being present compressed and expanded the fleeting elements of love, life and death into miniature movements that might in other genres of theatre be played out in a dramatic narrative depicting a specific situation.

The slow ontology of a performer such as Abramović has political significance because it 'initiates a performative critique of his or her participation in the general economy of mobility that informs, supports and reproduces the ideological formations of late capitalist modernity' (Lepecki 2006: 16). In Australia, the Yamatji artist Robyn Latham received permission from Abramović to use the structure of *The Artist Is Present* to stage a work called *The Aborigine Is Present* (2015) at the Koorie Heritage Trust Gallery in Melbourne: a table and two chairs, inviting individuals to sit and look at an Aboriginal Australian. In less demanding circumstances (shorter time and multiple performers) than Abramović gave herself, expectations of difference in appearance or life experience were challenged from both sides of the table. For some there were involuntary tears at recognition of the daily stereotyping of Aboriginal people, and for others there was the powerful experience of the right to affirm their identity in a supportive frame and public setting. In the calmness of the exchange, the quality of shared breathing, the movement of the heart in the chest and the silence between participants provoked some recognition of the enduring presence of Aboriginal people or, what Lara Stevens calls, 'life after extinction' (2018). Given the specificity of the Australian setting and the Aboriginal artist on one side of the table, Abramović's 'dramaturgy of stillness', neither leading anywhere in particular nor asking for action, allows the dust that accumulates in personal, cultural and colonial histories to be disturbed.

Slowness in contemporary theatre thus enables an important ontological shift in perspective. Paradoxically, it is the cessation of movement that releases energy and 'charts the tensions in the subject, the tensions in subjectivity under the force of history's dusty sedimentation of the body' (Lepecki 2006: 15). Durational theatre, or theatre that quietens time, will allow the inexorable slowness of the audience's historical imagination to hover and emerge in the shadows of representation. For Abramović and many of her participant visitors, the performance was a 'life-changing event'; for her it expanded the sense of community and the grave responsibility she had as an artist. What slow theatre draws attention to is not then the singularity of embodiment, but the performance of active and 'loving' observation exchanged between actor and audience in a common reality. The prevalence of works that seek co-presence in performance of which Abramović's example is one of many gives a double sense to this tenderizing, as in softening the sinews of meat or something fleshy, as well as the generation of a tender affect. Compositional strategies for using movement time to stop or slow experience also allow the audience insight into earlier performances – political resistance, historical events, domestic life and personal tragedy – which may become manifest as distinctive processes of transformation. Slow theatre may therefore include the non-virtuosic, the forgotten and the past imperfect within the present, which in turn reflects on the mortal fragility of societies and individuals in transition.

While performance time gives shape to a major dimension of theatre's encounter with the world, which the two preceding examples have shown may be either universalizing or deeply personal, the final two case studies will ground our theories of movement in terms of weight and meaning. With an overarching journey in this book organizing movement from the individual to the collective, via the techniques and methods of plasticity, effort and energetic intensity, the future of theatre will now be filtered by works that reimagine the aesthetics of animation and force.

Animation: *Blackie Blackie Brown* (2018)

Black performance theorists have radically extended the conception of the nomad to address the movements of diasporic identity for those groups who share common histories of geography or ethnicity but are widely dispersed. A diasporic identity may also be enacted and affirmed by communities who feel displaced from a dominant cultural ethos: '[D]iaspora is continual; it is the unfolding of experience into a visual, aural, kinesthetic culture of performance … [which] brings together collective experiences around particular issues, forces, or social movements' (DeFrantz and Gonzalez 2014: 11). Black performance theory has also shifted racialized discourse from one of negative subjectivity, the sense of being that lacks full selfhood, towards a critical stance on the dominance of whiteness (its myths, its characters and its bodies) in theatre and performance. As Thomas de Frantz and Anita Gonzalez assert, black performance theory is of necessity oppositional in its rejection of 'the timeworn death wish cast against black expression', but it also increasingly seeks to express the optimistic potentiality within blackness, whereby 'the senses actualize temporality, enliven desire, and embrace beauty across the poetics of bodies and the aesthetics of their creations' (2014: xviii).

The rejection of negative ontologies and the weight of history as limitations on black expression have been extended by concepts such as 'Afro-futurism' in which black writers and artists turn away from realist genres and other oppressive representations of capture and instead harness science fiction, fantasy and popular culture for the imagining of a black future. A significant feature of Afro-futurism is the interaction between embodied signs, musicality and technology, as Kodwo Eshun explains in his ground-breaking book on *Sonic Fiction*, such performance 'moves through the explosive forces which technology excites in us, the temporal architecture of inner space, audiosocial space, living space, where postwar alienation breaks down into the 21st century alien' (1998: 52). Movement, inasmuch as it retains an embodied dimension, is experienced then through the transference between technology that moves with rhythmic frequencies, and the subject of the black artist that moves to express the post-human by rejecting their dehumanized identity with fantasy. Literary scholar Ytasha Womack, in her writing on Afro-futurism, also calls for an aesthetics 'jettisoning into the far-off future, the uncharted Milky Way, or the depths of the subconscious and imagination' (2013: 2). So what does it mean to consider a proposition that movement in theatre may be escapist, playful and future-oriented in order to release non-white energies and imaginations?

Given my context of working in Australia, I want to pick up some of these tools of black performance theory to consider a theatre work created by Indigenous and queer artists working with a disjunctive but futurist aesthetics. In a colonial context, where race remains a key determinant of social outcomes, resistance to identity norms has been part of an everyday tactic of survival for Indigenous Australians, and their presence in urban environments busts open myths and histories that have previously defined 'primitive cultures'. Given millennia of territorial occupation, Indigenous knowledge of nomadism is not trapped in the past but has a powerful contemporary voice in 'Stories that offend my mother' as Australian Indigenous playwright Nakkiah Lui proclaimed on national radio in 2013.[2] Extending this concept as 'The Right to Offend', Indigenous visual artist Brook Andrew argues that Aboriginal artists need to overturn or problematize 'the velocity of dominant cultures, the velocity of an opinion, [which] reflects the outside voices of "You shouldn't do this and you should do that"' and I want to suggest here that such irreverence can be powerfully represented as movement towards the future (cited in Ryan 2017: 23).

In her dramaturgy for *Blackie Blackie Brown* (2018), Lui turns the logic of a timeless past upside down by creating a black superhero whose alter ego is the Aboriginal archaeologist Dr Jacqueline Black, a character identifying Aboriginal bones at a 'sacred site' at risk of being destroyed to build a factory. Having unearthed an ancestral skull which conjures up the power of her great grandmother's story of a truly brutal massacre, Dr Black subsequently transforms into the exuberant superhero Blackie Blackie Brown, played by Megan Wilding (2018) and Dalara Williams (2019) in a co-production for the Malthouse (Melbourne) and Belvoir Street Theatre (Sydney).

In a script that jumps from quick sketch to surreal scene, Blackie (a derogatory term for an Aboriginal Australian), hereafter referred to as BBB, decides then to take revenge on the living descendants of all the whites – doctors, tradesmen, shoppers, children – who were involved in the murder of her grandmother's tribal ancestors, as she shouts 'your white meat is DONE!'[3]

The intermediality of this innovative production leads movement analysis in new directions because much of the action is created through specific animation references and techniques, from stop-motion and flip-book animation, time-lapse, morphing, object transformations and computer-generated graphics. The sequences of cartoon animation interact with live action – literally BBB jumping against walls that scream 'Wham!, Kapow!' – and slapstick – such as comic chases down alleyways – which allow the superhero the full range of expletives, fights and escape tricks as she bashes and crushes all the other characters (played by actor Ash Flanders). Flanders is an experimental queer artist and his comic versatility skips across multiple stereotypes – from a gay man chatting to his boyfriend about what he is wearing in the gym and what he learnt about 'the serious theatre' from seeing the 'lovely skin' of Indigenous people; to a safari-suited boss working for In Vitro Inc, a corrupt company that sequences genomes in order to change Aboriginal women into white men; to the frightened hippie wife whose family ancestors were murderers – and his performance requires constant mutation of voice, body type and nervous energy.

Mediated by the animations projected on all surfaces of the stage, the physical interactions between BBB and the other characters are driven by the superhero goal of combatting the 'evil force of white injustice' and the virtual movement dramaturgy runs at a pace or rhythm counter to any naturalist rendition. For instance, when BBB finally agrees to take on her grandmother's crusade of revenge, she must get into training, and what follows is a sequence of rapid vignettes with rap soundtrack that are presented inside projected light boxes:

BBB on the running machine, BBB doing t'ai chi, BBB learning to box. Faster and faster, the actor cannot keep up with the grandma avatar that shadows her from frame to frame, and Wilding bends double with exhaustion: 'Oh, I'm going to be sick.' This disjunctive sign of the Indigenous body who does not want to compete, who is not perfectible, is accompanied by other disjunctives, such as bad-taste jokes about identity, spoken between the characters against Aboriginal Australians, but also in fair return against white society: 'What do you call a dead white man? Justice', says Dr Black, as she strips off her white gown, to reveal the pink BBB superhero costume, complete with black Madonna bra, Aboriginal flag waistband, blue hair and white batgirl eyes. The cartoon character then empowers a different sense of movement, which encompasses the BBB figure as an animation, that is not just 'the *movement*, that belongs, not to what is immediately seen to move, but to something that is itself seen to move *in the movement that is immediately presented*' (Malpas 2014: 69, italics in original). This last point about animation is that there is something 'in the movement', in addition to the visible movement, that has been moved.

Not bound by realism in scale or virtuosity, the fast pace and absurd situations of BBB's animated crusade therefore expose the white denial of Australia's racial history, and the blown-up violent gestures embody the antithesis of a black imaginary that lives with racial violence every day. This reconfiguring of movement potential projects forward and back in time simultaneously as it asks the viewer to consider how justice might be delivered for the wrongs of the past or the racism of the present? Such existential questions become, for BBB (and Indigenous Australians), part of the everyday experience of oppression in a racist society, that does not acknowledge Aboriginal sovereignty over land, nor the wrongs perpetrated by white Australia since colonization. Through animation, however, the Indigenous writer, artist and actor mobilize the fantastical; in doing so, they create the 'story of how apparent non-value functions as the creator of value' (Moten 2003: 18). Hands on hips, when BBB declares 'get ready to die' she challenges Flanders, now wearing the white Klu Klux Klan garment of an imagined Aussie Patriot. With psychedelic lighting, pink on vivid blue, the two hurl themselves around the stage in a cartoon fight complete with punches and kicks. Folding into each other with exaggerated howls of pain, BBB is slammed against the wall, and the Patriot jumps in the air, attacking her with an Australian flag on a pole. BBB has the superpower of a silver boomerang, whose cartoon replica ricochets across the walls like a bouncing ball, while BBB strips off the Patriot's KKK cloak revealing his shiny Aussie shorts, socks and sandals. He freezes in mid-run, and the slow-motion sequence includes more boomerang throwing, green lights, stick figures attacking and the slashing of his Achilles heel, with a dramatic spurt of orange-red blood spilling over the floor. The sequence melds body and prosthetic weapon – the flagpole, the boomerang – with body and technology – the fake blood and amplified sound effects. Pathetically reduced to begging, the Patriot protests, 'I have redeemable qualities', as she spears him with his own flagpole: 'Advance Australia Dead Mother Fucker'.

In Lui's *Blackie Blackie Brown*, the movement repertoire is 'deadly', an Aboriginal term that is affirmative of survival humour – geeky, blunt and big – as much as its production aesthetics are awkward, slippery and shocking, and uncomfortably funny. For instance, how should anyone react to a big inflatable plastic hammer bopping a series of caricatured white Australians on the head? This playful action lets Indigenous artists take a direct swipe at white society, although mercifully the superhero starts to doubt the path of repaying vengeance with more violence when her final victim helps save her from a ring of burning oil. The images hence, both embodied and virtual, are animated towards a different alignment of relations between reality and another as yet-unimagined reality. But the animation of these shocking ideas is itself a movement that inheres in the performance – catapulting hand to rhythmic motif or linking a picture of parliament to a racist news broadcast. The non-linear narrative and the animated video and lighting effects shift the perceptions of whose real exists, as the movements of the Indigenous actor and her camp partner exaggerate the banality of everyday racial ignorance. Like Jarry's brutal puppets in the 'pschittical' fantasy discussed in Section Two, an animation allows the performers to offend us by blustering and blocking our desire to naturalize them. While Simultaneously the animations of the Indigenous avenger propel forward the dramatic questions: will good win out? Should the bad be punished? When the anti-hero BBB cries out an answer, we listen acutely: 'They will hold justice away from us, at arm's length, forever, ... we need to awaken our power ... to make sense of the nonsense'.

The philosopher Jeff Malpas, writing on animation, makes the connection between Aristotle's notion of 'anima' with which we opened this book and the wonders of animation as a form of reflection on a naïve movement aesthetics; he writes that a 'making move' in animation connects 'with the emphasis on the "making" here (on *techne*), on a certain *art* of movement' (2014: 70). For him, there is movement that takes place in animated drawings, in cinematic figures, as well as in the spaces that unify the image with their reality. In this sense, animation engenders, and emplaces, the movement which propels the animated figure – to put it another way, the animations of BBB orient the spectator to an expanded experience of everyday Indigenous reality, by launching a big, bold, female superhero – a cosmic re-invention of Indigenous ancestral power – in motion.

Making an animated form of Indigenous theatre, the production of Blackie Blackie Brown plays thus across the lines of fantasy and reality in the movement of its game-like players. As the word 'white white' flashes on the wall, we see the animated BBB flying over the city as buildings explode. Kicking a cyclist wearing grey Lycra and zapping him with her laser sword, she wipes her brow with sweat as his mouth gushes into a green bile that covers the stage and nearly drowns her. The theatrical vision of Indigenous futurism thereby catapults the present into the viewpoint of a future in which the perspective of realism, and racist white society, has been extinguished. For black artists such as Eshun, Womack, Andrew and Lui, the contemporary practice of art-making by-passes theatre's claim to humanity, which it understands as a 'trap', within a racially constructed paradox of linear time and horizon (Womack 2013: 153). Rather than preach or depict the history of Indigenous experience, Lui's animation of physical absurdity and technological mischief thus produces a derisive and dangerous, but inclusive, laughter. In doing so, Indigenous theatre helps to make manifest the movement of an Indigenous futurity that black theorist Fred Moten predicts will be 'born not in bondage but in fugitivity, in stolen breath and stolen life' (2003: 305).

Force: *World Factory* (2014), *Made in Bangladesh* (2015), *World Factory* (2016)

For the final case study of contemporary theatre, I am returning to the attention I have given to collective social formations – choruses, processions and crowds. A key theorist for analysing movement as a social phenomenon is the postcolonial scholar Arjun Appadurai whose 1996 book, *Modernity at Large: The Cultural Dimensions of Globalisation*, was a compelling analysis of the many ways in which globalization has effected modern societies. His argument is structured around the concept of 'flows' or 'scapes' that are transnational movements of ideas, people and practices that have become pervasive in their influence and circulation upon the experience of everyday social life, and these 'scapes' include mediascapes, ethnoscapes, technoscapes, financescapes and ideoscapes, to which we might add corpo-scapes (the dimensions of embodiment). What is important about the 'scapes' of modern globalism is that they move, traversing boundaries of state and territory, and in the process, those 'scapes' shape ordinary people's awareness of their lived possibilities in patterns of production, consumption and imagination. What interests me in Appadurai's approach is the emphasis on micro-practices, such as the 'manipulability of the body' to become flexible and ephemeral; on the other hand, a 'scape' is also an ideological layer in the everyday that becomes normalized and durable (1996: 84). We love to eat chocolate, which is often now salted and dark so we are deluded into thinking we are 'more healthy' or superior to those who eat the cheaper dairy nut, but none of us think about the finite resources of cocoa and cane or the workers that facilitate these sugary desires. Appadurai's concern is that the mobilizing effects of global capital that allow us to enjoy chocolate, for instance, are harnessed by the power of state or capitalist forces into processes and forms of mobility that regulate our lives.

Many different theatre productions might illustrate one or other of the 'scapes', but rather than think of their formation as flows or fluid features of global modernity, an idea that has been critiqued by many scholars, I want to give the 'scape' a stronger movement definition by considering them as forces. Forces in physics change the motion of an object, but they also give magnitude and direction to a movement. In terms of movements that interact with bodies in social life and across the globe, forces are also uneven, free flowing at times and, at others, encountering resistance and blockages. Rather than one case study, given the emphasis here on global forces, I will introduce three works – from China, Bangladesh/Germany and the UK – that might be called community, radical or immersive theatre. Each of them examines the consumption of fashion, and its movement through bodies, exemplifying therefore a 'cultural dimension of globalization'.

Founded in 2005, Grass Stage is a Shanghai theatre collective, led by artistic director Zhao Chuan, that includes trained and untrained actors with careers in education, architecture, business, advertising and psychiatry. Their production *World*

Factory (2014) begins simply enough with a couple of 'clowns' cutting the heads from a string of paper dolls, because they seem unfit – lacking the physical or psychological resilience – for factory work: 'This one has a bent back! This one is too skinny and can't deal with overtime!' Rocking back and forth with laughter, the two performers offer fake tears, 'what a horrible society', as they look at the remnants of the paper bodies left on the floor.[4]

Like the other works in this section, the production is episodic with a collage of scenes that examine the history of the 'world factory' from its inception in Manchester in late eighteenth-century cotton mills through to today's global industrial complex operating in China and other parts of South and Southeast Asia. Dressed in everyday clothes, the unremarkable bodies of the performers contribute to its visual aesthetics, which as Zhao Chuan explains 'publicly demonstrate the identities, postures and manners of speaking of completely ordinary people, revealing a critical and deeply paradoxical relationship to the utterly deformed picture of reality long propagated by the state' (2018). Movement is orderly but mobilized to resist – they march up and down behind cardboard signs while chanting slogans 'about the bosses, laws and police, and clocks, that regularize our movements'. Later, speaking as 'workers' in blue shirts, we see a demonstration of the Taylorist time and motion, as mentioned in Section Two, that measured efficiency in modern industrial workplaces. With syncopated actions, the performers mime the assembly line; lifting, straightening, carrying, cleaving, turning knobs, and hammering – 'no sighs, no gaps, no breaks' allowed.

Demonstrating how capitalism has a history of industrial production to harness exploited labour at the cheapest possible price, one of the audience members is asked to come and skip rope, for which they will be paid '1 cent/jump', and while they jump, the actors calculate their value over a day of skipping. In the background of this short funny interlude, another female 'worker' is skipping slowly; she then turns more rapidly, jumping and jumping, as she tells of a nightmare in which she can't quite reach a boat leaving shore. Still skipping, she recounts working overtime for days, 'exhausted as if my body wasn't my own', and the feeling of a violent pain in head and stomach. Pausing for a moment to wipe her brow, she hesitates – should she keep on going? but she imagines her children leaving on the boat without her and starts skipping again with more momentum. The sense of fatigue, 'but my body won't move, it's sore and tired, it won't move', forced upon her by the exertions of skipping, or working, is accompanied then by an affective outcome; her body is worn out as much as she is dehumanized.

Given capital's exploitation of industrial labour flows, and the West's dependence upon China for its consumer products, the economic impact of such corporeal interactions becomes both a motif and a motive within this performance. At one side of the stage and throughout the performance are three actors seated at illuminated worktables. Quiet, regulated and efficient, one 'worker' folds sheets of blue paper, another cuts them first with a guillotine and then scissors, and a third stamps them back and front. The stencil cutting of the paper dolls continues, emulating smooth flow, while the next actor in line pegs them on ropes that crisscross the stage space; as these figures accumulate, however, they are jerked along, shaking and fluttering like flags. In their multitudes these uniform, faceless and flaccid paper bodies stand in for the hundreds upon hundreds of identical items that factory production demands, but also for the workers who make them, wherever they are, who are rendered disembodied and nameless by the transnational forces of factory production.

The countering of this situation emerges in the 'post-performance theatre' of the factories, schools and foyers of buildings in which GrassStage perform, with conversations that often last longer than the show. The audience, like them, is caught in the push and pull of desire that global commodities activate, whether it is to own the next best thing or simply to have the wage check that accompanies a kind of personal opportunity for betterment. The forces are contradictory, both individual and collective, and no one agency within the system moves without another.

This negative imagery of mass industry – its denial of freedom – contrasts with another work that also examines the scale and effects of global clothing production. *Made in Bangladesh* (2015) was created by the Berlin-based choreographer Helena Waldman in partnership with *kathak* teacher Vikram Iyengar and a company of *kathak* dancers in Dhaka, Bangladesh. Like GrassStage, Waldman undertook years of research to understand the global flows of consumption capitalism that structure the Western experience of 'merchandising, fashion and fantasy' which hide behind the dynamics of an industry designed around poor employment practices – factory collapses, toxic wastes, injured workers – in a country such as Bangladesh (Appadurai 1996: 81). With a strong focus on embodied movement, this dance theatre work signifies this labour with the rhythm of dancing feet, their metre pounding out the tike-tike-tak-tak pattern of *kathak* that replicates the sound of sewing machines. One German reviewer describes the transformations between body, action and machinic production with eloquence:

> [T]he dancers line up on stage, at first without showing their faces, colourfully clad from head to bare toe in Shalwar Kameez, wide long shirts, trousers, headscarves. They work. First with their feet only, the heels. Lift, lower, up, down. The knee slightly bent. The contact with the floor slowly becomes audible, the whole foot goes into action, taps then also at an angle, or steps to the side, and then back. Intermediate steps. They all become ever faster, the sole patter becomes music. Heads click to the side, hands get busy, the arms spell out the geometry of the Kathak: to the top, below, sideward, diagonally. Sometimes they look as if they are measuring lengths of cloth – endlessly repeated.
> (Suchy 2015)

The dancers not only represent the efficient machine, but they are also the skilled workers, whether artists or clothing producers, and while they keep pace with the requirements of dance director or factory boss, their bodies also participate in the paradoxical demands of 'modernity at large'. This parallel with performance adds a layer of contradictions to *Made in Bangladesh* about the effects of accelerated movement. In Waldman's ethnography of the female workers, she gives voice to women who are willing participants in the deterritorializing effects of capitalism; namely they desire to be part of the ethnoscapes and financescapes that will facilitate their escape from poverty or from domestic constraints. Paid only small amounts for their piecework 'fourteen hours on six days a week – for 2.50 Euros a month', they say, 'We are happy' and 'no boycotts please' (Suchy 2015). But as the production points out on an electronic scoreboard, the volume of items they produce makes the low cost of clothing sold in European shops seem scandalous.

In Appadurai's terms, the production fetishism that governs such wage labour 'masks translocal capital, transnational earning flows, global management and often faraway workers' reducing them to 'the idiom and spectacle of local (sometimes even worker) control, national productivity and territorial sovereignty' (1996: 42). The factory form disguises globally dispersed forces of capital consumption and those forces which demand local social compliance by alienating workers from any agency in the workplace. They also hide the state machinery – once Taiwan, then China, now Bangladesh – which is forced to keep moving in the ideoscapes and mediascapes of consumption that dominate the West.

An alternative tallying of the dynamics of global fashion production was theatricalized in a different version of *World Factory*, developed in partnership with Zhao by Zoë Svendsen and Simon Daw from the Cambridge performing arts company Metis. Presented in London in 2016 before touring and being published as a card game, this production took the form of an interactive event in which the audience is divided into groups that must become the 'managers' of the cyclical ebbs and flows as well as competitive demands of purchasing power in a Chinese clothing factory. Overseen by a series of actors who provide prompts, the audience is asked to simulate the experience of competing with other firms, hence stretching the limits of 'individual decision-making and systemic pressure'. A group at one table is, for instance, pitted against a series of 'wins' that can be made either by blaming and laying off workers to cut costs or by succumbing to the consumer desire for fast fashion in the global marketplace. The forces here are intense, competitive, with the agency of the audience driving the speed of transactions, but they are also forced to account ultimately for the apparent 'choices' each group has made by the night's end. The production format therefore provides an ethical re-enactment of the transnational movements embedded in the very clothes we wear.

In these three productions, the experience of force does not represent an individual's freedom to express themselves within a personal drama, but rather the performers embody the pulse and experience of commodity production itself. The *kathak* dancer, the Chinese worker, the textile garment-maker and the factory manager represent the accelerating components in a global machine of modernity that promises greater consumption while manufacturing desire. Appadurai's analysis of these cultural dimensions of mobility is therefore parlayed into these performances by virtue of theatrical devices that harness the rhythm of a movement system – the clattering feet, cutting fingers – and the technical discipline required by the system – the uniform blue-paper shapes, the repetitive sounds – as well as the fantasy of selfhood or freedom – breaking step, or breaking down, or breaking out. Each of these productions shapes questions about the forces that shape subjectivity as a form of social production, one that continues afterwards in dialogue with their audiences.

At the conclusion of World Factory in Shanghai, 'a masked, anonymous, seemingly lunatic character runs to the audience from the stage', as Zhao Chuan explains, 'Haha! If this turns out to be real, will you still be able to have iPhones? To prance about in designer brands? If that is what will happen, will your life be changed! Aren't you terrified? Do you want that? Aren't you scared? Do you want that?' (Zhao Chuan 2014). Another person responds by asking what it would be like to have a system in which there was no exploitation or minimal consumption: how would we change the movement-scapes that drive this global machine? In a brief manifesto, a group of contemporary Chinese theatre artists meeting at the Shanghai-based Institute for Provocation call their approach to theatre not a mode of expression but a process requiring 'submergence' in the history and politics of everyday cultural reality, which 'without capital' can be independent from state identity and its insistence on standardized methods of production. GrassStage as an example of such theatre, according to Zhang Xian, becomes 'unprecedently sensual and current to our cultural context, [by] creating a truthful relationship to our historical reality' (2018). Waldman is more ambivalent: 'Everyone has to decide for themselves how they respond to exploitation, I am an artist not an adviser' (Baumeister 2014), while Svendson and Daw suggest their theatrical provocation aims 'to reflect critically on what constitutes success in the system' (2017).

Such recent theatre productions affirm Appadurai's notion that the global flows of modernity transfer forces to the translocal experience of 'wanting, remembering, being and buying' so that the ontology of many different bodies, whether in theatre or dance, fashion or activism, becomes affected by the ephemeral demands of cultural production. The theatrical mediation of capitalist forces in these three recent works is perhaps one step towards an evolving 'postnational imaginary' that enables cultural producers, such as theatre artists, to embody and enact the social transformation of movement (Appadurai 1996: 177).

Conclusion

This final section has explored four ideas about movement in contemporary theatre: speed, slowness, animation and force. It has done this by examining a series of postdramatic works that depart from the text and which utilize the technological mediations of virtual and reproductive technologies within the formal structures of theatre's meaning-making apparatus. Their creators and audiences have, as the examples illustrate, been nomadic with ideas, techniques and practices that respond to the conditions of their times, and in turn they have imagined movement genres, patterns and styles for the theatre. This centrality of movement to theatre draws us, whether audience or actors, into our experience of the world, subtly and dynamically, and with varying levels of attraction and repulsion, mobilization and resistance.

Imagine an object, thing or person that is in one place and finds itself propelled, moved, towards another place, whether real or metaphorical. That movement will vary in speed or velocity, or be felt at varying scales and intensities, whether micro or macro, and in direction, upwards or downwards, forwards or backwards, and hence the object journeys through time in its own trajectory. But things do not move in isolation; instead they move in relation to things around them and they change one another in the process of moving. These experiences are those of the individual actor and, at the same time, those of the society or groups within a society. Their movements accumulate through repetition and are modified by the internal workings of the groups and by ideology, which is politics and, over time, which is what we call history.

If we return to Aristotle's thinking about movement with which this book began, movement could not be defined as physics, anima or poetics, but as some part of the phenomenon of the whole vitality of life. To put it differently, movement is also mechanics, energy and art, since modernity has added to these philosophical understandings of momentum, and we now have a greater sense of the social tensions and political differences as bodies experience displacement, temporality, weight and the force of events. It is through this sense of motion and the variable relations between subjectivity, theatrical ideas and creative projects that I invite readers of this book to make their own connections to the sense and excitement of movement ideas. Theatre is an unstable reality, shifting the shapes and dynamics of time, space and moving bodies. In the adaptations humans and other species make within the volatility of a finite and fragile world, none more so than theatre in movement.

NOTES

Movement: Introduction

1   *Songs of Childhood*, Concept and Choreography: Pascal
Merighi; Dance: Thusnelda Mercy and Dominique Mercy;
Text: *Song of Childhood* by Peter Handke; Reader: Jack
Laskey; Light designer: Adam Carree and Pascal Merighi;
Camera and Editing: Charly Cattrall. Originally commissioned
by Sadler's Wells, London, as part of Elixir Festival 2017.
https://vimeo.com/241251215 (accessed 27 July 2020).

Section One

1   All quotations taken from the Arden Shakespeare edition of *The
Tempest* (Shakespeare 2011).

Section Two

1   Verbal references are from the performance video of *Audience*,
viewed online, with all rights reserved to Ontroerend Goed.

Section Three

1   The production and file notes of *Attempts on Her Life* were
viewed at the National Theatre Archive, London, in January
2020. All rights reserved to the artists.

2   'Stories That Offend Your Mother: Nakkiah Lui' by Daniel
Browning on *AWAYE!*, ABC Radio, 31 August 2013. https://www.
abc.net.au/radionational/programs/awaye/awaye-anniversary-
lecture-nakkiah-lui/4881740 (accessed 27 July 2020).

3   Verbal references are from the performance video of *Blackie Blackie Brown*, viewed at the Malthouse Theatre with permission, and not Lui's script which is unpublished, with all rights reserved to Nakkiah Lui.

4   Verbal references are from the performance video of *World Factory*, OCAT, Schenzhen, November 2014, viewed online and uploaded to Vimeo by Seachina, with all rights reserved to GrassStage.

REFERENCES

Movement: Introduction

Aristotle (1996). *Physics*. Ed. D. Bostock and trans. R. Waterfield. New York: Oxford University Press.

Aristotle (2017). *De Anima*. Trans. C. D. C. Reeve. Indianapolis: Hackett Publishing Company.

Carlson, M. (1984). *Theories of the Theatre: a Historical and Critical Survey from the Greeks to the Present*. Ithaca and London: Cornell University Press.

Hoghe, R. (2016). *Bandoneon: Working with Pina Bausch*. London: Oberon Books.

Lefebvre, H. (2004). *Rhythmanalysis: Space, Time and Everyday Life*. London: Bloomsbury.

Mauss, M. (1979). *Sociology and Psychology: Essays*. Trans. B. Brewster. London: Routledge.

Meyer, M. (2017). *Pina Bausch: Dance, Dance, Otherwise We Are Lost*. London: Oberon Books.

Peponi, A.-E. (2013). 'Theorizing the Chorus in Greece', in J. Billings, F. Budelmann and F. Macintosh (eds), *Choruses, Ancient and Modern*, 15–34, Oxford: Oxford University Press.

Section One: Movement as History

Aristotle (1996). *Poetics*. Trans. M. Heath. London: Penguin.

Aristotle (2017). *De Anima*. Trans. C. D. C. Reeve. Indianapolis: Hackett Publishing Company.

Babo, J. M. (1801). 'Otto of Wittelsbach: Or, the Choleric Count. A Tragedy in Five Acts', in A. W. Iffland, F. Schiller and J. W. Von Goethe (eds), *The German Theatre*, Vol. 4. London: Vernor and Hood.

Barish, J. A. (1981). *The Antitheatrical Prejudice*. Berkeley: University of California Press.

Bharata, M. (1950). *The Natyasastra: A Treatise on Hindu Dramaturgy and Histrionics*. Trans. M. Ghosh. Calcutta: Asiatic Society.

Billings, J., F. Budelmann and F. Macintosh (eds) (2013). *Choruses, Ancient and Modern*. Oxford: Oxford University Press.

Brown, J. R. (2005). *Shakespeare Dancing: A Theatrical Study of the Plays*. Basingstoke, Hampshire: Palgrave Macmillan.

Butler, J. (2006). *Gender Trouble: Feminism and the Subversion of Identity*. New York and London: Routledge.

Coppola, A. (2016). *The Theater of Experiment: Staging Natural Philosophy in Eighteenth Century Britain*. Oxford: Oxford University Press.

Darwin, C. (1880). *The Power of Movement in Plants*. London: John Murray.

Diderot, D., and J. le R. d'Alembert (2003). 'Senses' and 'Automaton', in N. S. Hoyt and T. Cassirer (trans.), *The Encyclopedia of Diderot and d'Alembert Collaborative Translation Project*, Vol. 15 (1765), 24–7 and Vol. 1 (1751), 896–7, Ann Arbor: Michigan Publishing, University of Michigan.

Dürrenmatt, F. (1973). *The Visit: A Tragi-Comedy*. London, Cape.

Fischer-Lichte, E. (2008). *The Transformative Power of Performance: A New Aesthetics*. London: Routledge.

Gotman, K. (2018). *Choreomania: Dance and Disorder*. Oxford: Oxford University Press.

Greenblatt, S. (1980). *Renaissance Self-Fashioning: From More to Shakespeare*. Chicago: University of Chicago Press.

Gurr, A. (1996). *The Shakespearean Playing Companies*. Oxford: Clarendon Press.

Harvey, W. (1628). *The Anatomical Exercise, Concerning the Motion of the Heart and Blood*. London: Frances Leach.

Jarry, A. (1965). *Alfred Jarry: The Ubu Plays*. Ed. S. W. Taylor. London: Methuen.

Jonson, B. (1838). *The Works of Ben Jonson*. London: Edward Moxon.

Keenan, S. (2014). *Acting Companies and Their Plays in Shakespeare's London*. London: Bloomsbury.

Von Kleist, H. (1972). 'On the Marionette Theatre'. Trans. T. G. Neumiller. *The Drama Review: TDR, The Puppet Issue* 16.3: 22–6.

Latham, J. A. (2015). 'Inventing Gregory "the Great": Memory, Authority, and the Afterlives of the *Letania Septiformis*'. *Church History* 84.1: 1–31.

Lavater, J. C. (1866). *Physiognomy, or, the Corresponding Analogy between the Conformation of the Features and the Ruling Passions of the Mind: Being a Complete Epitome of the Original Work of J.C. Lavater*. London: William Tegg.

Markley, A. A., and M. L. Wallace (eds) (2016). *Re-Viewing Thomas Holcroft, 1745–1809: Essays on His Works and Life*. London: Routledge.

Marshall, C. W. (2006). *The Stagecraft and Performance of Roman Comedy*. Cambridge: Cambridge University Press.

Mehl, D. (1965). *The Elizabethan Dumb Show: The History of a Dramatic Convention*. London: Methuen.

Mitra, R. (2015). *Akram Khan: Dancing New Interculturalism*. London: Palgrave Macmillan.

Northbrooke, J. (1843). *A Treatise against Dicing, Dancing, Plays and Interludes*. London: The Shakespeare Society.

Oosterwijk, S., and S. Knöll (2011). *Mixed Metaphors. The Danse Macabre in Medieval and Early Modern Europe*. Newcastle-upon-Tyne: Cambridge Scholars Publishing.

Peponi, A-E. (2013). 'Theorizing the Chorus in Greece', in J. Billings, F. Budelmann and F. Macintosh (eds), *Choruses, Ancient and Modern*, 15–34, Oxford: Oxford University Press.

Plato (2014, 1926). *Laws, Book 2*. Trans. R. G. Bury. Loeb Classical Library. Cambridge, MA: Harvard University Press.

Quintilian (2001). *The Orator's Education*. Trans. D. A. Russell. Cambridge, MA: Harvard University Press.

Ristvit, L. (2015). *Ritual, Performance, and Politics in the Ancient Near East*. New York: Cambridge University Press.

Roach, J. (1985). *The Player's Passion: Studies in the Science of Acting*. Ann Arbor, MI: University of Michigan Press.

Rubin, D., C. S. Pong, R. Chaturvedi, R. Majundar and M. Tanokura (eds) (2001). *The World Encyclopedia of Contemporary Theatre: Asia/Pacific*. London: Taylor and Francis.

Salazar-Sutil, N. (2015). *Motion and Representation: The Language of Human Movement*. Cambridge, MA: MIT Press.

Salazar-Sutil, N., and S. Popat (eds) (2015). *Digital Movement: Essays in Motion Technology and Performance*. London: Palgrave Macmillan.

Sawday, J. (2007). *Engines of the Imagination: Renaissance Culture and the Rise of the Machine*. London: Routledge.

Shakespeare, W. (2011). *The Tempest*. Eds V. M. Vaughan and A. T. Vaughan. London: Bloomsbury.

Smethurst, M. (2011). 'Are We All Creons and Ismenes? *Antigone* in Japan', in E. B. Mee and H. P. Foley (eds), *Antigone on the Contemporary World Stage*, 1–14, Oxford: Oxford University Press.

Smethurst, M. (2013). *Dramatic Action in Greek Tragedy and Noh: Reading with and beyond Aristotle*. New York: Lexington Books.

Smith, A. (2004). *Selected Philosophical Writings*. Ed. J. R. Otteson. Exeter, UK and Charlottesville, VA: Imprint Academic.

Sophocles (1959). 'Antigone', in D. Grene and R. Lattimore (eds), *The Complete Greek Tragedies*, 157–206, Chicago: University of Chicago.

Stafford, N. (2007). *War Horse: Adapted for the Stage from the Novel by Michael Morpurgo*. London: Faber.

States, B. O. (1985). *Great Reckonings in Little Rooms: On the Phenomenology of Theater*. Berkeley: University of California Press.

Strong, R. C. (1973). *Splendour at Court: Renaissance Spectacle and Illusion*. London: Weidenfeld and Nicolson.

West, S. (1991). *The Image of the Actor: Verbal and Visual Representation in the Age of Garrick and Kemble*. London: Palgrave Macmillan.

Wright, D. (2004). *I Am My Own Wife*. New York: Alexander Street Press.

Zeami (1984). *On the Art of the Nō Drama: The Major Treatises of Zeami*. Trans. J. T. Rimer and M. Yamazaki. Princeton: Princeton University Press.

Zeami (2008). *Zeami: Performance Notes*. Trans. T. B. Hare. New York: Chichester, Columbia University Press.

Section Two: Movement Systems and Embodied Action

Allain, P. (2017). 'Grotowski: Interview with Paul Allain'. *Essential Drama: Thinking Together about Theatre*. http://essentialdrama.com/practitioners/grotowski/ (accessed 27 July 2020).

Artaud, A. (1970). *The Theatre and Its Double*. Trans. V. Corti. London: Calder and Boyars.

Baird, B. (2012). *Hijikata Tatsumi and Butoh: Dancing in a Pool of Gray Grits*. London and New York: Routledge.

Bergson, H. (1991). *Matter and Memory*. Trans. N. M. Paul and W. S. Palmer. New York: Zone Books.

Boenisch, P. M., and T. Ostermeier (2016). *The Theatre of Thomas Ostermeier*. London: Routledge.

Braun, E. (2016). *Meyerhold on Theatre*. London: Methuen.

Brecht, B. (1962). *Mother Courage and Her Children*. London: Eyre Methuen.

Brecht, B. (1978). *Brecht on Theatre*. Trans. J. Willett. London: Eyre Methuen.

Broinowski, A. (2017). *Cultural Responses to Occupation in Japan: The Performing Body during and after the Cold War*. London: Bloomsbury Academic.

Brook, P. (2009). *With Grotowski: Theatre Is Just a Form*. Wroclaw: The Grotowski Institute.

Canetti, E. (1981). *Crowds and Power*. Harmondsworth: Penguin.

Churchill, C. (2008). *Top Girls*. Eds B. Naismith and N. Worrall. London: Bloomsbury Publishing.

Cima, G. G. (1993). *Performing Women: Female Characters, Male Playwrights, and the Modern Stage*. Ithaca, NY: Cornell University Press.

Craig, G. (1977). *Gordon Craig on Movement and Dance*. Ed. A. Rood. London: Dance Books.

Crespi, P. with S. Manghani (2015). 'Rhythmanalysis: An Interview with Paola Crespi'. *Theory, Culture & Society*, 13 May, online. https://theoryculturesociety.org/rhythmanalysis-an-interview-with-paola-crespi/ (accessed 27 July 2020).

Diamond, E. (1988). 'Brechtian Theory/Feminist Theory: Toward a Gestic Feminist Criticism'. *TDR: The Drama Review* 32.1 (Spring): 82–94.

Fensham, R. (2019). 'Affective Spectatorship: Watching Theatre and the Study of Affect', in C. Stalpaert, K. Pewny, J. Coppens and P. Vermeulen (eds), *Unfolding Spectatorship: Shifting Political, Ethical and Intermedial Positions*, 39–62, Ghent: Academia Press.

Foster, S. L. (2011). *Choreographing Empathy: Kinesthesia in Performance*. London: Routledge.

Garner, S. B. (1994). *Bodied Spaces: Phenomenology and Performance in Contemporary Drama*. Ithaca: Cornell University Press.

Grosz, E. (1994). *Volatile Bodies: Toward a Corporeal Feminism*. Sydney: Allen and Unwin.

Grotowski, J. (1968). *Towards a Poor Theatre*. London, Methuen.

Johnston, D. (2017). *Theatre and Phenomenology: Manual Philosophy*. London: Palgrave.

Jones, D. R. (1986). *Great Directors at Work: Stanislavsky, Brecht, Kazan, Brook*. Berkeley: University of California Press.

Kelleher, J. (2015). *The Illuminated Theatre: Studies on the Suffering of Images*. London: Routledge.

Laban, R. (2011, 1950). *The Mastery of Movement on the Stage*. Hampshire: Dance Books.

Laban, R. (2014). 'Eurhythmy and Kakoryhthmy in Art and Education'. Trans. P. Crespi. *Body and Society, Special Issue: Rhythm, Movement, Embodiment* 20.3&4: 75–8.

Maletic, V. (1987). *Body, Space, Expression: The Development of Rudolf Laban's Movement and Dance Concepts*. Berlin: Walter de Gruyter.

McKenzie, J. (2001). *Perform or Else: From Discipline to Performance*. New York: Routledge.

Merleau-Ponty, M. (2004). *Maurice Merleau-Ponty: Basic Writings*. Ed. T. Baldwin. London: Routledge.

Muybridge, E. (1955). *The Human Figure in Motion*. New York: Dover.

Nietzsche, F. (1996). *Philosophy in the Tragic Age of the Greeks*. Washington, DC: Regnery Publishing.

Ohno, K., and Y. Ohno (2004). *Kazuo Ohno's World: From Within and Without*. Trans. J. Barrett. Middletown, CT: Wesleyan University Press.

Pitches, J. (2003). *Vsevold Meyerhold*. London: Routledge.

Preston, C. J. (2011). *Modernism's Mythic Pose: Gender, Genre, Solo Performance*. New York: Oxford, Oxford University Press.

Roesner, D. (2016). *Musicality in Theatre: Music as Model, Method and Metaphor in Theatre-Making*. London: Ashgate.

Rudnitsky, K. (1981). *Meyerhold, the Director*. Ann Arbor: Ardis.

Schmidt, P. (1996). *Meyerhold at Work*. New York: Applause.

Shawn, T. (1974). *Every Little Movement: A Book about Francois Delsarte*. Brooklyn, New York: Dance Horizons.

Stanislavski, C. (1950). *Building a Character*. London: Max Reinhardt.

States, B. O. (1985). *Great Reckonings in Little Rooms: On the Phenomenology of Theater*. Berkeley: University of California Press.

Stebbins, G. (1977). *Delsarte System of Expression*. New York: Dance Horizons.

Styan, J. L. (1982). *Max Reinhardt: Directors in Perspective*. Cambridge: Cambridge University Press.

Toepfer, K. (1997). *Empire of Ecstasy: Nudity and Movement in German Body Culture, 1910–1935*. San Francisco: University of California Press.

Whyman, R. (2008). *The Stanislavski System of Acting: Legacy and Influence in Modern Performance*. Cambridge: Cambridge University Press.

Young, I. M. (1990). *Throwing Like a Girl and Other Essays in Feminist Philosophy and Social Theory*. Bloomington: Indiana University Press.

Section Three: Movement for Contemporary Theatre

Abramović, M. (2016). *Walk through Walls*. New York: Crown Archetype.

Appadurai, A. (1996). *Modernity at Large: Cultural Dimensions of Globalization*. Minneapolis: University of Minnesota Press.

Baumeister, U. (2014). 'Helpless but Moved'. *Badische Neueste Nachrichten*, 5 December. https://www.helenawaldmann.com/works/madeinbangladesh/ (accessed 27 July 2020).

Beckett, S. (1984). *Worstward Ho: Beckett Shorts Vol. 4*. London: Calder Press.

Benjamin, W. (1992). 'The Work of Art in the Age of Mechanical Reproduction', in *Illuminations*, 217–51, London: Fontana.

Bhabha, H. (1984). 'Of Mimicry and Man: The Ambivalence of Colonial Discourse'. *October* 28 (Spring): 125–33.

Braidotti, R. (1994). *Nomadic Subjects: Embodiment and Sexual Difference in Contemporary Feminist Theory*. New York: Columbia University Press.

Bryden, M. (2004). 'Beckett and the Dynamic Still'. *Samuel Beckett Today* 14: 179–92.

Butler, J. (2006). *Gender Trouble: Feminism and the Subversion of Identity*. New York: Routledge.

Causey, M. (2006). *Theatre and Performance in Digital Culture*. London: Routledge.

Chuan, Zhao. (2014). 'Sentiments in the Age of Consumerism', in *OCAT Performs: Program*. Shenzhen, November.

Chuan, Zhao. (2018). 'Theatre of a Different Kind'. *Prohelvetia*. Zurich. https://prohelvetia.ch/en/artist/chuan-zhao/ (accessed 27 July 2020).

Crimp, M. (1997). *Attempts on Her Life*. London: Faber and Faber.

DeFrantz, T., and A. Gonzalez (2014). *Black Performance Theory*. Durham and London: Duke University Press.

Deleuze, G., and F. Guattari (1987). *A Thousand Plateaus: Capitalism and Schizophrenia*. Minneapolis: University of Minnesota Press.

Eshun, K. (1998). *More Brilliant than the Sun: Adventures in Sonic Fiction*. London: Quartet Books.

Lavender, A. (2010). 'Digital Culture', in S. Bay-Cheng, C. Kattenbelt, A. Lavender and R. Nelson (eds), *Mapping Intermediality in Performance*, 125–34, Amsterdam: Amsterdam University Press.

Lehmann, H.-T. (2006). *Postdramatic Theatre*. London: Routledge.

Lepecki, A. (2006). *Exhausting Dance: Performance and the Politics of Movement*. London: Routledge.

Malpas, J. (2014). 'With a Philosopher's Eye: A "Naïve" View on Animation'. *Animation: An Interdisciplinary Journal* 9.1: 65–79.

Moten, F. (2003). *In the Break: The Aesthetics of the Black Radical Tradition*. Minneapolis: University of Minnesota Press.

Redhead, S. (2004). *Theorist for an Accelerated Culture*. Edinburgh: Edinburgh University Press.

Ryan, J. with B. Andrew (2017). *The Right to Offend Is Sacred*. Melbourne: National Gallery of Victoria.

Salazar-Sutil, N., and S. Popat (eds) (2015). *Digital Movement: Essays in Motion Technology and Performance*. London: Palgrave Macmillan.

Sierz, A. (2007). 'Program Notes', in *Attempts on Her Life*. Program viewed London: National Theatre Archive, January 2020.

Stevens, L. (2018). 'Life after Extinction'. *Performance Research* 23.3: 27–36.

Suchy, M. (2015). *Helena Waldmann: Made in Bangladesh*. Berlin: TANZ, May. https://www.helenawaldmann.com/works/madeinbangladesh/ (accessed 27 July 2020).

Svendson, Z., and S. Daw (2017). *World Factory: The Game*. London: Nick Hern Books.

Virilio, P. (2003). *Art and Fear*. London: Continuum.

Virilio, P. (2010). *The Futurism of the Instant: Stop-Eject*. London: Polity.

Womack, Y. (2013). *Afrofuturism: The World of Black Sci-Fi and Fantasy Culture*. Chicago: Chicago Review Press.

Xian, Zhang with Yang Meiqi, Wen Hui, Tian Gebing, Xiang Shixi, Cao Kefei, and Song Yi (2018). 'Autonomous Theatre and Rewriting Theatre History'. Trans. S. Lu. Living Dance Studio, Paper Tiger Studio, and Niao Collective in collaboration with Beijing Inside-Out Art Museum. Institute for Provocation, 16–17 December.

FURTHER READING

In addition to expanding your reading from the key references, if you would like to explore more ideas relating to movement in theatre, here are some key texts to help you make a start.

Movement philosophy

Stanton B. Garner, *Kinesthetic Spectatorship in the Theatre: Phenomenology, Cognition, Movement* (London: Palgrave Macmillan, 2018). Garner's latest book extends the focus on movement perception from classical phenomenology to more contemporary approaches to theatre, such as theories of kinaesthesia, empathy and cognition. It usefully extends the philosophy of mind to a diverse range of theatre examples including disability aesthetics, puppetry and spectatorship.

Tim Ingold, *Being Alive: Essays on Movement, Knowledge and Description* (London: Routledge, 2011). Ingold's poetic and philosophical approach to spatial anthropology often features reflections on movement as a social, cultural or environmental practice. This volume with its focus on 'being alive' is no exception, with essays that range across the experience of handwriting, to walking and storytelling as a spatial practice.

Alva Noë, *Action in Perception* (Cambridge, MA: MIT Press, 2004). For a contemporary philosopher's take on the cognitive turn in studies of movement, perception and aesthetics, any of Noe's recent books are generative, accessible texts for understanding how neuroscience is engaging with consciousness. See also *Strange Tools: Art and Human Nature* (New York: Hill and Wang, 2015) where he engages explicitly with the complexity of choreographic thinking as a form of philosophy.

Philipa Rothfield, *Dance and the Corporeal Uncanny: Philosophy in Motion* (London: Routledge, 2020). With a focus primarily on dance, but with insights extending to performance and cultural studies, the philosopher Rothfield unpicks with characteristic lucidity the significance and agency of corporeal thinking that is embedded in theories of phenomenology and the philosophies of Nietzsche and Deleuze.

Performance Philosophy https://www.performancephilosophy.org/ journal (accessed 27 July 2020) is a disciplinary journal with new thinking from hermeneutics, post-structural theory, process philosophy and phenomenology. The journal includes many articles on movement for topics relating to practice-as-research, dance, somatics, Butoh, rhythm, expression and aesthetics.

Theatre history

Karen Brazell, *Traditional Japanese Theatre: An Anthology of Plays* (New York: Columbia University Press, 1999). This valuable volume introduces histories of traditional theatre in Japan and includes translated scripts from a selection of Noh plays, as well as discussion of techniques of staging including the movement of musicians, actors and props. Accompanied by a range of resources about Noh theatre available online http://www.the-noh.com/ (accessed 27 July 2020), this collection provides source materials for attempting to move Noh scripts into performance.

Susan Leigh Foster, *Choreographing Empathy: Kinesthesia in Performance* (London: Routledge, 2010). Foster's book provides an intellectual history for concepts that are influential in movement theory in contemporary performance, such as kinaesthesia, empathy and somatics, dating them back to the physical education movements of the late nineteenth century. She also discusses how gender, class and race shape the role of movement ideas in higher education and dance reception.

George Rodosethenous, *Contemporary Adaptations of Greek Tragedy* (London: Bloomsbury, 2017). This collection of essays provides insight into the many ways in which Greek tragedy continues to be influential in theatre. While historical in a more recent sense, its transnational approach expands knowledge of Greek theatre history with discussion of directors, also referenced by the current volume, such as Katie Mitchell, Jan Fabre, and Japanese directors Tadashi Suzuki and Yukio Ninagawa.

Movement training

Michael Chekhov, *To the Actor: On the Technique of Acting*. (San Francisco: Muriwai Books, 2017). The New York Acting Studio, established by Chekhov, has built upon the legacy of the Russian theatrical experiments in 'psycho-physical' acting techniques, but while lesser known, his method builds explicitly on Laban's concepts of movement qualities in the kinesphere, and the use of effort to support dynamics, thus extending European nineteenth-century thinking about movement to the twentieth century for the American theatre profession.

Deborah Hay, *My Body the Buddhist* (Middletown, CT: Wesleyan University Press, 2000). This book, written twenty years ago by the expert practitioner and teacher Hay, accounts for the philosophical learning that comes from bringing consciousness to movement as a source of dance, theatre and performance. Like Dalcroze and Laban's influence as movement theories in the mid-twentieth century, this book paved the way for twenty-first-century reflections on somatics as a movement methodology.

Jacques LeCoq, *Theatre of Movement and Gesture*. Ed. David Bradby (London: Routledge, 2006). This influential theatre educator has trained generations of contemporary performing artists, such as the actor Geoffrey Rush and director Simon McBurney, with his approach to corporeal mime, and he has a well-articulated philosophy of movement as a physical language.

Mabel Todd, *The Thinking Body* (New York: Dance Horizons, 1937). This is a seminal text for basing knowledge of movement in anatomy and for articulating the concept of ideokinesis, the sense of images shaping how we adjust inner movement. Her book has informed many developments in movement education, such as Pilates, that we now call somatics.

There are many hundreds of books on movement techniques and training methods in theatre studies, but for a sample of current ideas, the journal *Theatre, Dance and Performance Training* (https://www.tandfonline.com/toc/rtdp20/current, accessed 27 July 2020) has well-argued essays documenting and analysing movement techniques from the historical record as well as contemporary methods and practices.

Decolonizing movement

S. S. Barlingay, *A Modern Introduction to Indian Aesthetic Theory* (New Delhi: Printworld, 2016). Contemporary writing on classical Indian performance theory is difficult to find; this book is quite technical but usefully explains the concept of *rasa* and *abhinaya* (the bodily movements and facial changes of acting) in chapter-length discussions.

F. Moten, *In the Break: The Aesthetics of the Black Radical Tradition* (Minneapolis: University of Minnesota Press, 2003). While Moten's book is briefly referenced in the current volume, its importance for thinking about black performance genres and aesthetics needs to be highlighted. With a semiotic methodology, Moten argues for a conception of radical politics that occurs in the cut or 'break' opened up in the rhythms of poetry, music and visual arts in black cultural practices.

Glenn A. Odom, *World Theories of Theatre* (London: Routledge, 2017). This book contains a useful collection of short excerpts from global approaches to theatre that are otherwise difficult to locate, such as from the Natyasastra or Zeami's Noh aesthetics. It provides schematic introduction to a wide range of contexts, although some of the extracts are old translations and should not be relied on uncritically.

Carrie Sandahl and Phillip Auslander, *Bodies in Commotion: Disability and Performance* (Minneapolis: University of Michigan Press, 2005). This edited volume thinks of disability performance as a 'commotion' that is unruly as well as a 'co-motion' or 'moving together' which is enabled by the theatrical experiences and affects of performance by differently abled bodies. The collection includes essays by seminal writers in the field, such as Petra Kuppers, whose own book, *Disability and Contemporary Performance* (New York: Routledge, 2003), provides a philosophical overview of disability performance as well as personal accounts of building community through theatre.

INDEX